المَوْلِدُ الدِّيبَعِي

Mawlid al-Dība[c]ī

With commentary by Sheikh [c]Alawī al-Mālikī

Al-Imām al-Jalīl [c]Abd al-Raḥmān al-Dība[c]ī

SAKINA

ISBN 978-0-9566146-1-2

Published by Sakina, UK
Previously known as Sandal Books

www.sakinapublishing.com

Author: Al-Imām al-Jalīl ᶜAbd al-Raḥmān al-Dībaᶜī
Commentary: Sheikh ᶜAlawī al-Mālikī
Translation: Rizwana Sayed

1st Edition

Printed in Great Britain

بسم الله الرحمن الرحيم

Contents

Acknowledgements

With utmost respect and honour, I would like to thank my Sheikh, Sheikh Muhammad Sadiq ᶜAlawī, who instructed and authorised for this work to be carried out. I was only able to accomplish this through his noble teachings, blessings and dua. May Allah increase his life, so that he may continue in the footsteps of his blessed Master and Sheikh, Sayyidinā Ḥabīb Aḥmad Mashhūr Al-Ḥaddād رضي الله عنه*, calling people to Allah and guiding them towards the Messenger of Allah* ﷺ.

Translator's Introduction

In the Name of Allah, the All-Compassionate, the All-Merciful
Praise be to Allah, the One Who created the light of the noble Prophet, and may the most exalted blessings and peace be upon His Chosen One, Sayyidinā Muḥammad.

Praise of the Prophet ﷺ has been an intrinsic part of Islam from its very beginning. Initially this was expressed in the Sublime Words of Allah the Exalted, accentuating the excellence of the Prophetic character: "*Indeed you are of an exalted disposition*"[1] "...*Indeed you are upon the straight path*"[2] "*We have only sent you as a mercy to the worlds.*"[3] Thus indicating a platform reserved solely for this noble Prophet, such praises had not been conferred to anyone before and demonstrated in the Divine Word.

Thereafter, the verses of praise were elaborated at the hands of the noble Companions as they witnessed and observed exceptional qualities emerging from the noble Prophet of Allah. The short simple Qur'ānic verses in Prophetic praise transformed into longer and elaborate verses of poetry. The

---

[1] Qur'ān, 68:4
[2] Qur'ān, 43: 43
[3] Qur'ān, 21: 107

admiration of the Companions was expressed in short compositions:

'A trustworthy one, chosen, calling to goodness,

Resembling the light of the full moon detached from darkness.'[4]

[Sayyidinā Abū Bakr al-Ṣiddīq ﷺ]

'If you were anything other than a human being,

you would be the light on the night of a full moon.'[5]

[Sayyidinā ᶜUmar ibn. al-Khaṭṭāb ﷺ]

Sayyidinā ᶜAbbās ﷺ, the uncle of the noble Prophet ﷺ said: "O Messenger of Allah I wish to praise you." He ﷺ replied: "Go ahead, may Allah adorn your mouth with silver!" The last two verses of his poem:

'And then when you were born, a light rose over the earth until it illuminated the horizon with its radiance. We are in that illumination and that original light and those paths of guidance, and thanks to these we pass through.'[6]

---

[4] Al-Ḥaddād, Ḥabīb ᶜAlawī ibn Aḥmad, *Miṣbāḥ al-Anām wa Jalā' al-Ẓalām fī Radd Shubah al-Bidᶜī al-Najdī,* trans. Ḥaddād G. F., P.225

[5] Ibid.

[6] Ibid., P.222

When he ﷺ left Makka and emigrated to Madina, Sayyida cAtīka bint cAbd al-Muṭṭalib, the aunt of the noble Prophet recited:

> *'My eyes have overflowed with streaming tears shed for the Uniquely Chosen One, the Full Moon of the House of Ḥāshim.'*[7]

And also expressed in longer compositions, such as the famous masterpieces by Kacb ibn al-Zuhayr, Ḥassān ibn Thābiṭ, Kacb ibn Mālik and cAbdallāh ibn al-Rawāḥa. Ḥassān ibn Thābit, served the Prophet ﷺ with his poetry in Medina. His verses in praise of the Prophet would extol his spiritual virtues, his religious mission, and enumerate the graces bestowed on him by Allah. Moreover, the veneration illustrated in his verses shows the impact this had upon their faith:

> *'I witness with God's permission that Muhammad is the Messenger who is higher than heaven.'*[8]

The famous *Bānat al-Sucād* by Kacb ibn al-Zuhayr ؓ elicited the forgiveness and pleasure of the blessed Prophet to the extent that he granted him his own mantle as a gesture of happiness.

Hence, great significance was given to venerating the Messenger of Allah ﷺ by those whose lives were touched by him. The Prophet's expressions of happiness and rewards were treasured and contended for, since they indicated a means, whereby the pleasure of Allah could be acquired and His wrath drawn away. Not only was it the beauty in physique and character that enthralled all those who encountered him but it

---

[7] Ibid. p. 225

[8] Cf. Schimmel, A.M., *And Muhammad is his Messenger*, p. 179.

was also on realising the intimacy between Allah and His Messenger that indicated a prestigious rank, which was to be honoured or it would impair one's faith. "…*Those who harm the Messenger of Allah, for them there is a painful torment*",[9] and "*Allah will not punish them while you are amongst them*",[10] "*Say, if you love Allah then follow me, Allah will love you and forgive you your sins*".[11]

Even after the noble Prophet left this world, compositions in his praise and veneration continued, however it was now poetry in yearning for his presence and for a glimpse of his beauty. Their desire to be in his presence incited them to devote their lives in collating and composing devotional works about the noble Prophet ﷺ. Thus, their compositions would include the unrivalled features of his noble personage, life and creation that accentuated his nobility over others. Such as the primacy of his creation, the immaculate lineage, the signs of Prophethood as manifested before the noble birth and on its advent, and the occurrence of exceptional events as witnessed by the Companions, but foremost dedication would be towards mentioning the exquisite form and demeanour of the Prophet. The verses of many eminent poets illustrated that despite their many words in Prophetic praise, they were yet unable to do justice to his worth. As the notable scholar Yūsuf Nabhānī expresses:

> *They say to me, "Did you not praise Muḥammad,*
> *The Prophet of the God of all things created,*
> *The most worshipable amongst men?"*
> *I said to them, "What shall I say in his praise*
> *Since his Creator has praised him and has not left anything to say?"*[12]

---

[9] Qur'ān, 9: 61
[10] Qur'ān, 9: 33
[11] Qur'ān, 3:31
[12] Cf. Schimmel, A.M., *And Muhammad is his Messenger*, p. 177

And Lisānuddin ibn al-Khaṭīb says:

> *'The verses of the Holy Book have praised you, so how could the poem of my eulogy possibly praise your greatness?'*[13]

And similarly the eminent Imām Busīrī, in his *Hamziyya* says:

> *'Is it not the true miracle of the Prophet that tongues are incapable of describing him? Is not his praise like an unfathomable ocean without a shore, which the divers cannot measure out?'*[14]

Despite this dilemma faced by many theologians and poets, their hearts longed to mention his noble name and qualities in alliance to their oft quoted saying: "It belongs to the nature of the lover to mention the beloved constantly."[15]

The present work composed by ᶜAbd al-Raḥmān ibn Muḥammad al-Shaybānī enumerates the aforementioned themes and presents them in the form of a *mawlid*.[16] The *mawlid* opens with the praise of Allah, followed by the creation of the noble Prophet, may blessings and peace be upon him, thereafter he mentions the blessed birth, the miraculous events and the numerous virtues of the Prophetic character, as cited in the Ḥadīths.

---

[13] Schimmel A.M. *And Muhammad is His Messenger*, p. 177

[14] Ibid.

[15] Ibid.

[16] '*Mawlid*', the word which denotes the day of birth, it became a technical term specific to the Prophet's birthday as the festivities of this day increased during the late Middle Ages, the term is especially applied to the poetry or literature written in honour of the Prophet ﷺ

Historical background

Celebrations in memory of the Prophetic birth or *mawlid*, on a large scale seem to have first emerged during the Fatimid era (969/1171) in Egypt. Such occasions, in which sermons were delivered, sweets circulated and alms distributed to the poor were usually attended by scholars and religious authorities. However, it was not long before these sober and pious gatherings attracted the masses, whereby celebrations became more elaborate. As celebrations of the *mawlid* spread throughout the Islamic lands, local and common practices merged within the religious occasion. Such practices caught the attention of orthodox scholars, who attacked the celebrations that were infiltrated with rituals, which contradicted Islamic measures.

Indeed the scholars of the 13th and 14th centuries, by their censure of innovative practices were trying to maintain the religious grounds for such gatherings and were opposed to those occasions that became an event for entertainment and light-headed amusement. They were not, however against the initial purpose of the *mawlid*, since it was as mentioned earlier, inaugurated by the scholarly elite. Moreover, one of the earlier works on *mawlid* that is almost exclusively composed of Ḥadīth is ascribed to Ibn Kathīr, the disciple of Ibn Taymiyya.[17]

With the upsurge of attacks and rebuke against the festive occasion, eminent scholars of the 15th and 16th centuries, such as Imām al-Suyūṭī and Ibn Ḥajar al-Ḥaythamī clarified all misconceptions by producing works in defence of the 'good innovation'. These works provided authoritative guidelines, distinguishing the permissible acts from the impermissible. Henceforth, compositions of the *mawlid* and the festive

[17] Ibn Taymiyya (d. 1328), the theologian, who especially attacked the infiltration of popular practices within mainstream Islam.

occasion assumed a more orthodox character; and works in defence of the *mawlid*, proliferated over the years.

Content and format

The text that has been translated here is the *mawlid* of the Imam ^{c}Abd al-Raḥmān al-Dība^{c}ī, a mawlid which is well known and loved in the Muslim world. This particular text has been translated alongside a commentary by the contemporary scholar the *muḥaddith* from Makkah, Muḥammad ibn ^{c}Alawī ibn ^{c}Abbās al-Mālikī. He begins his commentary with an introduction that sets forth an account on the validity and the merits of gathering for the commemoration of the Prophetic birth. Being a Ḥadīth scholar (*muḥaddith*), Sheikh Muḥammad ibn ^{c}Alawī al-Mālikī examines all the Ḥadīths cited in the *mawlid*, illustrating the grade of their authenticity. Hence he sets forth an appraisal that allows the reader to see the basis of the poetic verses and distinguish the words of Ḥāfiẓ ^{c}Abd al-Raḥmān al-Dība^{c}ī from the words of the noble Prophet ﷺ. The footnotes have been differentiated between the comments of the translator (marked with a letter) and the comments of the esteemed scholar Shaykh ^{c}Alawī (marked with a number).

For practical usage the book has been double sided. The text leading from the front is the English translation with the Arabic and the text leading from the back is just the Arabic. It is customary in many countries to recite the *Salutations before the mawlid* (page 85) before the actual recitation of the mawlid itself. Furthermore, upon arriving at the moment of the description of the birth of the Prophet of Allah ﷺ it is customary to stand in honour of the momentousness of that occasion and to recite the chapter on the *Greetings for the Prophet* (page 88) whilst standing.

Muḥammad ibn ᶜAlawī al-Mālikī al-Ḥasanī

Muḥammad al-Ḥasan ibn ᶜAlawī ibn ᶜAbbās ibn ᶜAbd al-ᶜAzīz al-Mālikī was born in Makka. The early part of his studies took place in Makka under the instruction of his eminent father al-Sayyid ᶜAlawī al-Mālikī, who was more commonly known as the Imām of the Ḥaram. Thereafter, Imām Muḥammad ibn ᶜAlawī travelled to many countries in pursuit of knowledge, amongst these were North Africa, Egypt, India, Pakistan, Indonesia, the Philippians, where he gathered many works, encountered notable scholars, acquired knowledge of the Islamic sciences especially Ḥadīth and thereby he received many authorisations to teach.

His profundity in the Ḥadith sciences led him to compose many works on the subject, in addition to this, he has made a significant contribution to areas such as theology, law (*fiqh*), sufism (*taṣawwuf*) and *sīra*. He has composed over fifty works, such as '*Fī Riḥāb al-Bayt al-Ḥaram'*, which is a study on the Ḥadiths of Makka, and all matters related, and '*Al-Insān al-Kāmil*', the famous work on the demeanour of the noble Prophet, may blessings and peace be upon him. Moreover, he has produced significant works on the Muwaṭṭa of Imām Mālik and he has also written a commentary on the *mawlid* of Mulla ᶜAlī Qārī. Sheikh Muḥammad ibn ᶜAlawī passed away on the 15th of Ramadan 1425AH and he is buried in the al-Mualla cemetery in the sacred city of Makka. May Allah have mercy upon him.

Introduction by Sheikh Muḥammad ibn ᶜAlawī al-Mālikī al-Ḥasanī

In the name of Allah the most Beneficent the most Merciful. Praise be to Allah, Lord of the worlds, may blessings and peace be upon the most noble Messenger, our master Muhammad and upon his family and Companions.

ᶜAbd al-Raḥmān ibn ᶜAlī ibn Muḥammad al-Shaybānī ﷺ was Yemeni by descent and a follower of the Shafiᶜī school of thought. He was known by the name Ibn al-Dībaᶜī,[18] after his grandfather, al-ᶜAlā ibn Yūsuf. Ibn al-Dībaᶜī was born in the month of *Muḥarram,* [19] in the year 866 A.H, and he passed away on Friday 12th Rajab [20] 944 A.H.

He, may Allah have mercy upon him, held a unique position during his time. Many scholars of Ḥadīth are attributed to him and he was known to have related Bukhārī over a hundred times. Moreover, he had repute for his honest

[18] The literal meaning of *Dībaᶜī* is 'white'.

[19] *Muḥarram:* the first month of the Muslim calendar.

[20] *Rajab:* the seventh month of the Muslim calendar.

disposition, his eloquence and sweet manner in converse. Many works have been ascribed to his name, one of the most famous: *'Taysīr al-Wuṣūl ila Jamīᶜ al-uṣūl min Ḥadīth al-Rasūl'* which is a three volume work and also contains this noble mawlid.

In his introduction, Muḥammad ibn ᶜAlawī ibn ᶜAbbās al-Mālikī al-Ḥasanī, the author of the commentary on this mawlid, enumerates the many virtues contained in the recitation of the Prophetic mawlid. He states:

‘Much has been mentioned on the celebration of the Prophetic mawlid, therefore, I did not wish to elaborate on the topic further, for the reason that I feel along with many other scholars that this topic is greater than simply having it reduced to these nonessential issues. These have been treated thoroughly and dealt with at great length at every gathering and repeated every year to the extent that this kind of speech has now become tiresome for the people. However, it was only after the request of many of my brothers to be acquainted with my opinion in this field that I have decided to write on the topic. I request Allah the Exalted that all will savour the reward therein, āmīn.

Before I embark upon relating the proofs of celebrating and gathering for the noble mawlid, I would like to mention the following points:

In relation to its permissibility, we say that it is a gathering to listen to his noble *Sīrah*[21], may blessings and peace be upon him, and the praises that are mentioned in his worth, so that delight may enter the hearts of his *ummah*.

---

[21]*Sīrah:* literally means biography, however, it is now largely applied as the technical term used for the Prophet’s biography.

Regarding the one who believes in appointing the gathering for a particular day, we say that they have innovated in the religion. That is because one's remembrance and attachment to the Prophet ﷺ should be at all times. Indeed, during the month of his birth there is greater incentive to call and gather the people, in order to arouse their feelings by uniting them with that time, so that they may recall the past and shift from the seen into the unseen.

These gatherings are a great means to call the people to Allah; it is a golden opportunity not to be missed. In fact the scholars and propagators of the religion should revive the remembrance of the holy Prophet ﷺ with mention of his noble character, mannerisms, his various states, his *Sīrah*, his social interaction and his noble manner of worship. They should counsel and guide towards good and caution against tribulations, innovations, evils and affliction. By the grace of Allah when we participate in calling people to Allah, we say to them: 'The purpose of these gatherings is not merely in the interest of convening a gathering, rather it is a noble way towards a noble end… One who has not derived benefit therein, for the welfare of his religion, indeed he has been deprived of the blessings of the Prophetic mawlid.'

Evidences in relation to the celebration of the birth of the noble Prophet ﷺ.

Celebration of the Prophetic birth is a way of expressing joy and happiness for the holy Prophet ﷺ whereby, even the unbeliever has derived benefit. As has been reported in Bukhārī that every Monday the torment is lightened for Abū Lahab. This came as a result of his dismissal of Thawbiya, his female servant, when she gave glad tidings of the noble birth of the Prophet ﷺ. In light of this, Ḥāfiẓ Shams al-Dīn Muḥammad ibn Nāṣir al-Dīn al-Dimashqī writes in verse:

> *'If he was an unbeliever, whose censure was stated, "May his hands perish in the hellfire eternally!"* [22]
>
> *It came that every Monday, forever, it is lightened upon him for the delight of Aḥmad.*
>
> *Then, what is thought about the one, who throughout his life was delighted with Aḥmad,*
>
> *And died on the testimony of true faith.'*

The noble Prophet ﷺ is glorified on the day of his birth, wherein, appreciation is shown to Allah the Exalted for His great blessing upon him and for endowing him with a unique existence, and all those present manifest their joy. He ﷺ would express the delight of this honour by fasting as related in the Ḥadīth of Abū Qatāda: "The Messenger of Allah ﷺ was asked about fasting on Monday's. He replied: "On that [day] I was born, and on [that day] I received revelation."[23] Hence, the above illustrates the concept of celebration, however, there are various guises to the celebration, and therefore, the essential understanding remains equally, be it in the form of fasting, distributing food, gathering to remember him, recount his noble virtues, or invoking salutations upon him, may blessings and peace be upon him.

---

[22] Qur'ān, 111:1, the verse has been abridged for poetic use.

[23] Cited in Ṣaḥīḥ Muslim in the 'Book of Fasting'

According to Qur'anic ordainment, delight for the Messenger of Allah ﷺ is a requirement: "*Say for the favour of Allah and His mercy let them rejoice.*"[24] Thus Allah has enjoined rejoicing for His mercy, and the noble Prophet ﷺ is the greatest mercy; and Allah the Exalted said: "*We have only sent you as a mercy to mankind.*"[25]

The noble Prophet ﷺ used to observe particular days in association with significant bygone religious events. So, when a day of significance comes to pass we should use the opportunity to mention the event therein, and venerate it. He ﷺ himself established this principle as illustrated in the Ḥadīth: "When he ﷺ arrived at Madīna and saw the Jews fasting on the day of ᶜAshūra,[26] he asked them regarding this. It was said to him: 'They fast because they received salvation from God and their opponents were drowned; so it is a fast out of gratitude to God for this favour.' Then he ﷺ said: "We have a greater right over Moses than you." So he fasted and prescribed it too.[27]

Celebration of the mawlid was not a practice in evidence during the time of the Messenger of Allah ﷺ therefore, it is an innovation, however, it is a praiseworthy innovation for it falls under the rubric of the *sharīᶜah* and fulfils all the principles therein. It is an innovation with respect to its social aspect, not by virtue of its intention, for its purpose was present during the Prophetic era, as we shall set forth, by Allah's will.

---

[24]Qur'ān, 10: 58

[25]Qur'ān, 21: 107

[26]*Ashūra:* the tenth day of Muḥarram

[27] Cited in Ṣaḥīḥ Bukhārī and Muslim

The blessed mawlid arouses the desire to invoke blessings and peace upon him in adherence to the statement of the Exalted: "Verily Allah and His angels invoke blessings upon the Prophet, O you who believe invoke blessings upon him and salute him with a goodly salutation."[28] How much benefit and succor there is with invoking blessings upon him, the pen falls short in elucidating the impact of its many effects and the various phases of light therein.

The mawlid includes the mention of his noble birth, miracles, and acquaintance of his biography. So, are we not obliged to acquire knowledge of him, is it not binding upon us to live in compliance to him, emulate his noble actions, believe in his miracles and attest to his signs? Hence, it is the books of the mawlid that wholly fulfill this purpose.

To induce the rewards therein, by performing some of our obligations towards him, like illustrating his characteristics of perfection and his virtuous disposition. The poets used to dedicate their poetry to him, may blessings and peace be upon him, whereupon he would manifest his happiness with their work and reward them with kindness and blessings. Hence, if his pleasure was in evidence with those who praised him, how can his displeasure be the result of those who enumerate his noble traits? Indeed approximation to the Prophet is present by calling for his love and pleasure.

Knowledge of his noble traits, miracles and signs evoke perfection of faith in him, and an increase in love for him, may blessings and peace upon him. It is by virtue of human nature that a person is naturally affected by the love of beauty present in one's form and

---

[28]Qur'ān, 33: 57

nature, by one's knowledge and action, in one's state and belief. And we find that there is none more beautiful, or perfect, or virtuous than his blessed person ﷺ. Therefore, an increase in love and perfection in faith are two significant demands of the *sharī^{c}ah*, and naturally that which incites the two factors would prove to be a necessity too.

Exaltation of him ﷺ has been ordained. To rejoice on the day of his honourable birth by expressing joy through arrangement of feasts, gatherings of *dhikr* and honouring the poor are the most explicit ways of exaltation, expressing delight, joy and gratitude to Allah for the one through whom He has guided us.

Derived from his saying ﷺ regarding the excellence of Friday and the favours promised therein. On this day Adam عليه السلام which establishes the fact that the birthday of any prophet can be commemorated, may peace be upon them all. Then, what about the day when the best of prophets and the most noble of messengers was born?

This veneration should not only be singled out for the day of his birth, rather it should be dedicated to him, and oft repeated in a general way, just like Friday, which is commemorated out of gratitude for the favour bestowed [by Allah] and it is expressed for the virtues bestowed upon the Prophet, in revival of the most significant historical events, which possess the process of a significant reform in human history and the dawn of a new era. Just as days gain reverence, similarly locations acquire veneration with the birth of a prophet therein. Jibrīl, peace be upon him instructed the Prophet ﷺ to pray two units of prayer at Bethlehem, thereafter he said: "Do you know where you have prayed?" He replied in the negative, then Jibrīl said: "You have prayed in Bethlehem where ^{c}Īsā was born."

The mawlid is a practice, to which the scholars and the Muslims of all the countries have held a favourable opinion, and it is carried out in every region. It is a practice required by the *sharīᶜah* when analysed in light of its precepts, and by virtue of the reliable Ḥadīth (*mawqūf*) of Ibn Masᶜūd: "What the Muslims have regarded commendable is commendable with Allah and what the Muslims have deemed reprehensible is reprehensible with Allah."

Indeed the mawlid is a congregation of *dhikr*, charity, praise, and reverence for the Prophet, therefore, it is a sunna. These aspects are demanded by the *sharīᶜah* and are considered praiseworthy actions, as mentioned and urged in many sound Prophetic Traditions.

Allah the Exalted has said, "*And all that We recount to you of the stories of the Messengers is in order that We make your heart firm thereby.*"[29] This verse illustrates that the wisdom in relating the events of the Messengers, may peace be upon them, was to strengthen his noble heart. Then, inevitably we today need to strengthen our hearts with the recounting of their stories and events. And the most essential one is the mention of the blessed Prophet ﷺ.

An action not practiced by the pious predecessors, or found to be current in the first century does not necessitate it being a reprehensible innovation, nor does it qualify as sufficient basis to be denied or classified as a forbidden action. Rather the newly introduced matter should be scrutininsed in the light of legal proofs together with the rules regarding social welfare

[29] Qur'ān, 11: 120

enforced by the *sharīᶜah.* This is obligatory, for if the action is founded on the reprehensible, then it remains reprehensible, and if it is based on the permissible, then it is regarded permissible, if it is based on the recommended then it is classed as recommended. Thus, the means form the eventual ruling of the matter intended, and therefore, the scholars classified innovated matters into five categories:

- The **obligatory** (*wājib*), examples such as the rejection of the people of deviation, and the learning of Arabic grammar.

- The **recommended** (*manḍūb*), such as the building of schools, establishing the call to prayer on the pulpits, which were not practices of the first century.

- The **undesirable** (*makrūh*), such as the embellishment of mosques, and the adornment of the *muṣḥafs* (the copies of the Qur'ān).

- The **permissible**, (*mubāḥ*), such as the use of sieves, and elaboration in food and drink.

- The **reprehensible** (*ḥarām*), this would include all newly introduced matters that contravene the Prophetic Sunna, and do not have a sound basis in the *sharīᶜah.*

Therefore, not every innovation is blameworthy were it so, we would find that matters newly introduced by the Companions would be deemed unlawful; such as the compilation of the Qur'ān by Sayyidinā Abū Bakr, Sayyidinā ᶜUmar, and Sayyidinā Zayd ibn Thābit, (may Allah be pleased with them all), who implemented this fearing its loss with the passing away of many Companions, that had possessed it in memory.[30] Another example would be the initiation of Sayyidinā ᶜUmar ﷺ in his gathering people for prayer [*tarāwīḥ*] with one imām, wherewith he said: "What a praiseworthy innovation this is." And also the compiling of the useful sciences. In addition to this, the call to prayer on the pulpits would be forbidden as well as the founding of schools, institutes, hospitals, prisons, orphanages and aid agencies.

As a result, the scholars, may Allah be pleased with them, have limited the hadith: "Every innovation is misguidance" to the blameworthy innovation. And with this limitation, they explain all the events that occurred in relation to the most distinguished Companions and their Successors with respect to the newly introduced matters that were not in effect during the life of the blessed Prophet ﷺ. We, today have introduced many matters that were not embodied by the pious predecessors, such as the congregation of people behind an imam to perform the *tahajjud* prayer during the last part of the night after the *tarāwīḥ* prayer, and the completion of the Qur'ān therein. Followed by the recitation of the supplication of completing the Qur'ān, as well as delivering the *khuṭba* in the *tahajjud* prayer

[30]The compilation of the Qur'ān, in a Ḥadīth: 'Zayd ibn Thābit related that the Prophet ﷺ passed away and the Qur'ān had not been compiled anywhere. Then, (Sayyidinā) ᶜUmar ﷺ suggested to (Sayyidinā) Abū Bakr ﷺ the compilation of the Qur'ān in one book, after a large number of Companions were martyred in the battle of Yamāma. (Sayyidinā) Abū Bakr wondered, "How can we do something that the Prophet did not do?" (Sayyidina) Umar said, "By Allah it is good." He persisted in asking (Sayyidinā) Abū Bakr until Allah expanded his chest for it, and he sent for Zayd ibn Thābit and asked him to compile the Qur'ān. (Sayyidinā) Zayd ﷺ said, "By Allah if they had asked me to move a mountain it would not have been more difficult than to compile the Qur'ān." He also asked, "How could you do something that the Prophet did not do?" (Sayyidinā) Abū Bakr ﷺ replied, "It is good, and ᶜUmar kept returning to me until Allah expanded my chest in regard to this matter." Cited *Ṣaḥīḥ Bukhārī*

on the seventh and the twentieth night. And a proclaimer calling "*Ṣalāt al-Qiyām athābakumullāh*",[31] as all of these actions were not performed by the Messenger of Allah ﷺ or by any of the pious predecessors, hence, would these actions of ours be considered as blameworthy innovations?

Imām al-Shāfiᶜī ؓ said: "The innovation that contravenes the Qur'ān, the sunna, and scholarly consensus, is a devious innovation, while the innovation of good, that does not contravene any of the above is praiseworthy. Imām ᶜIzz ibn ᶜAbd al-Salām, al-Nawawī and Ibn al-Athīr hold the same opinion and have divided it into classes similar to the aforementioned.

All matters that are based on the principles of *sharīᶜah*, without any contradiction or blameworthy features therein are deemed as part of the religion. As for the opinion of the narrow-minded, who say that the pious predecessors did not implement that particular action, then their claim does not stand as sufficient proof. In fact, their claim has no evidence whatsoever; their case is like the one who has not studied the principles of the religion. However, with respect to an innovation of guidance, [i.e. the bringing about of a practice that draws one nearer to Allah], the scholars of *sharīᶜah* have regarded it as a sunna, and there is a promised reward for the one who initiates it. The Messenger of Allah ﷺ has said: "One who introduces a praiseworthy matter in Islam that is practiced after him, receives the reward of those who act upon it and nothing is diminished from his reward."

---

[31] 'The prayer is starting, may Allah reward you'

The event of the mawlid revives the remembrance of the Chosen one ﷺ and this is an obligation in Islam. Indeed, you may notice that many of the prescribed obligations of the hajj are a revival of praiseworthy events that were witnessed and of locations that behold blessings. The running between mounts *Ṣafā* and *Marwa*, the casting of stones and the sacrifice at *Minā* are all actions of bygone events. In commemoration of these events the Muslims revive the external aspect of these acts in the present day.

All the aforementioned points are considered from a legal perspective. Therefore, the mawlid is only sound when it is devoid of the blameworthy and the reprehensible. In the case of a mawlid that involves such acts, then it must be repudiated. Such examples are: the free mixing of men and women, the performance of reprehensible actions, excessive spending on things that would earn the displeasure of the one in whose memory the mawlid is held, may blessings and peace be upon him. Then, there is no blame in the prevention of such a gathering due to the blameworthy features involved. However, prohibition is in relation to its external aspect and not to its essential nature, which is not concealed to those who reflect.

The opinion of Sheikh ibn Taymiyya regarding the Mawlid

He said:

> "Some people are rewarded on performing the mawlid…" "And that which some people innovate by analogy with the Christian's who celebrated the birth of Jesus عليه السلام or out of love for the Prophet and to exalt him

> ﷺ Allah may reward them for this love and endeavour, but not on the fact that it is an innovation..."[32]

He further said:

> "Know that actions which involve good by virtue of the many obligations that are fulfilled therein, but also contain an innovation that is reprehensible, then such deeds are rendered blameworthy, as it contravenes the religion. Such is the case of the hypocrites and the transgressors, and is also evident from many in the *ummah* of the end of times. Therefore, you must be certain of two aspects. Firstly, that you seek adherence with the sunna inwardly and outwardly, and be aware of the good and refrain from evil; this applies to yourself, and anyone who follows you.
>
> Secondly, that you attempt to call people to the sunna as much as possible. If you see one who is acting upon the sunna yet he commits an undesirable action, then do not command him to abandon this, as it may result in his abandoning an obligatory or recommended act which is a greater wrong.
>
> If however, there is some sort of good in the innovation then compensate it, as much as possible with a good action that is established within the *sharīᶜah*, for it is human nature that one will only abandon a thing in exchange for another. And no one should abandon a good action except for an equivalent, or for an act better than it."

---

[32] An excerpt from his *fatwa*, from the book: '*Majmaᶜ Fatāwa Ibn Taymiyya*', Vol. 23, p.133.

He then said:

> "As for the veneration of the Prophet's birth with its performance in the season, as some of the people are doing, is good and there is great reward for the good intention and reverence for the Messenger of Allah ﷺ."[33]

---

[33] '*Iqtidā al-Ṣiraṭ al-Mustaqīm*', p.294-295.

"The noble Prophet ﷺ is present in every mawlid at the time of standing except in the Mawlid al-Dībaᶜī, verily he is present therein from beginning to end."

Ḥabīb Aḥmad Mashhūr al-Ḥaddād ؓ

بسم الله الرحمن الرحيم

اَلْحَمْدُ لِلّٰهِ الْقَوِيِّ الْغَالِبِ ۝ اَلْوَلِيِّ الطَّالِبِ ۝

اَلْبَاعِثِ الْمَانِحِ الْوَارِثِ السَّالِبِ ۝

All Praise belongs to Allah, the All-Powerful, the Overpowering, the Benefactor to the seeker, the One Who resurrects, bestows, inherits, and withholds.

عَالِمِ الْكَائِنِ وَالْبَائِنِ وَالزَّائِلِ وَالذَّاهِبِ ۝

يُسَبِّحُهُ الْآفِلُ وَالْمَائِلُ وَالطَّالِعُ وَالْغَارِبُ ۝

He Who has knowledge of the creation: the manifest, the transient and the fleeting. [All things that] set, incline, rise, and depart glorify Him.

وَيُوَحِّدُهُ النَّاطِقُ وَالصَّامِتُ وَالْجَامِدُ وَالذَّائِبُ ۝

يَضْرِبُ بِعَدْلِهِ السَّاكِنُ ۝ وَيَسْكُنُ بِفَضْلِهِ الضَّارِبُ ۝

He Who has knowledge of the creation: the manifest, the transient and the fleeting. [All things that] set, incline, rise, and depart glorify Him.

(لا إله إلا الله) حَكِيمٌ أَظْهَرَ بَدِيعَ حِكَمِهِ وَالْعَجَائِبَ ۝

فِي تَرْتِيبِ تَرْكِيبِ هَذِهِ الْقَوَالِبِ ۝

There is no god but Allah, Who is Wise. He manifests the splendor and wonders of His Wisdom in an arrangement and structure of these forms.

خَلَقَ مُخًّا وَّعَظْمًا وَّعُضَلًا وَّعُرُوقًا وَّلَحْمًا وَّجِلْدًا ۝

وَّشَعْرًا وَّدَمًا بِنَظْمٍ مُّؤْتَلِفٍ مُتَرَاكِبٍ ۝

He created the brain, the bones, the muscles, the veins, flesh, skin, hair, and blood, in a harmonious and imbricate system.

مِنْ مَاءٍ دَافِقٍ يَّخْرُجُ مِنْ بَيْنِ الصُّلْبِ وَالتَّرَآئِبِ ۝

(لا إله إلا الله) كَرِيمٌ بَسَطَ لِخَلْقِهِ بِسَاطَ كَرَمِهِ وَالْمَوَاهِبِ ۝

From a spurting fluid emerging from between the backbone and the breastbone.[34]

There is no god but Allah, the One Who is Generous, and extended the spread of His Generosity and His Favors for His creation.

يَنْزِلُ فِي كُلِّ لَيْلَةٍ إِلَى السَّمَاءِ الدُّنْيَا ۝

وَيُنَادِي : هَلْ مِنْ مُسْتَغْفِرٍ ، هَلْ مِنْ تَائِبٍ ۝

Every night He descends to the lowest heaven, and proclaims: "Is there anyone who seeks forgiveness? Is there anyone who seeks pardon?

هَلْ مِنْ طَالِبِ حَاجَةٍ فَأُنِيلَهُ الْمَطَالِبَ ۝ فَلَوْ رَأَيْتَ الْخُدَّامَ

قِيَامًا عَلَى الْأَقْدَامِ وَقَدْ جَادُوا بِالدُّمُوعِ السَّوَاكِبِ ۝

Is there anyone who seeks a need? I will fulfill his request."[35]

If only you had seen the servants standing on their feet with their tears flowing,

[34] Qur'ān, 86:7

وَالْقَوْمَ بَيْنَ نَادِمٍ وَتَائِب ۞ وَخَائِفٍ لِنَفْسِهِ يُعَاتِب ۞

وَآبِقٍ مِنَ الذُّنُوبِ إِلَيْهِ هَارِب ۞

And the people between remorse and repentance fearful, for that they may
be admonished. They escape from their sins and to Him they flee,

فَلَا يَزَالُونَ فِي الْإِسْتِغْفَارِ حَتَّى يَكُفَّ كَفُّ النَّهَارِ

ذُيُولَ الْغَيَاهِب ۞ فَيَعُودُونَ وَقَدْ فَازُوا بِالْمَطْلُوب ۞

they continue to seek forgiveness until daylight appears and darkness fades.
They return, victorious, with their needs [fulfilled]

وَأَدْرَكُوا رِضَا الْمَحْبُوب ۞ وَلَمْ يَعُدْ أَحَدٌ مِنَ الْقَوْمِ وَهُوَ خَائِب

(لَا إِلَهَ إِلَّا اللهُ) فَسُبْحَانَهُ تَعَالَى مِنْ مَلِكٍ أَوْجَدَ نُورَ نَبِيِّهِ

And they discern the pleasure of their Beloved. Not one of them returned
disappointed. There is no God but Allah, glory be to Him. From His
dominion He created the light of His Prophet,

---

[35] Derived from the sound Ḥadīth: "Our Lord, (Blessed and Exalted is He) descends
to the lowest heaven, every night, when the last third of the night remains, He says:
"One who calls upon me, I will respond to them, one who implores with me I will
grant them, one who seeks forgiveness with me, I will forgive them." Cited in
Bukhārī in the 'Book of Tahajjud'.

سَيِّدِنَا (مُحَمَّدٍ) صَلَّى اللهُ عَلَيْهِ وَسَلَّمَ

قَبْلَ أَنْ يَّخْلُقَ آدَمَ مِنَ الطِّيْنِ اللَّازِبِ ۝

Sayyidinā Muhammad ﷺ before He created Adam from sticky clay.[36]

وَعَرَضَ فَخْرَهُ عَلَى الْأَشْيَاءِ وَقَالَ: هَذَا سَيِّدُ الْأَنْبِيَاءِ

وَأَجَلُّ الْأَصْفِيَاءِ وَأَكْرَمُ الْحَبَائِبِ ۝

Then, He exposed His pride over all things, and said: "This is the master of all the prophets, the most eminent of the favoured and the most noble of the beloved.[37]

---

[36] This refers to the famous Ḥadīth related on the authority of Jābir ibn ᶜAbdallāh رضي الله عنه who said: "O Messenger of Allah, may my father and mother be your ransom, inform me of the first thing that Allah created, before all things." He replied, "O Jābir, Allah the Exalted created the light of your Prophet from His light before all things…" Narrated by ᶜAbd ar-Razzāq al-Ṣanaᶜānī and also cited in '*Al-Mawāhib al-Ladunniyya*'. The scholars are at variance regarding this Ḥadīth, some hold it to be authentic and others refute it.

[37] Al-Khatīb Baghdādī relates that (*Sayyidā*) Āmina رضي الله عنها said, "When I gave birth to him, I heard a herald proclaim: 'Circumambulate Muhammad in the East and the West and expose him to every spiritual body of the Jinn, the humans and the angels…' Ḥāfiz Qasṭalāni said that Abū Nuᶜaym has related it on the authority of Ibn ᶜAbbās, however, some do not hold it to be authentic.

اَللّٰهُمَّ صَلِّ وَسَلِّمْ وَبَارِكْ عَلَيْهِ

O Allah send peace and blessings upon him

قِيلَ: هُوَ نُوحٌ ، قَالَ: نُوحٌ بِهِ يَنْجُو مِنَ الْغَرَقِ

وَيَهْلِكُ مَنْ خَالَفَهُ مِنَ الْأَهْلِ وَالْأَقَارِب ۝

'It was asked, 'Is it Nūḥ?' Nūḥ said,[38] "By him, I was saved from drowning, and the disobedient amongst my people and family were destroyed."

قِيلَ: هُوَ إِبْرَاهِيمُ ، قَالَ إِبْرَاهِيمُ: بِهِ

تَقُومُ حُجَّتُهُ عَلَى عُبَّادِ الْأَصْنَامِ وَالْكَوَاكِب ۝

It was asked, 'Is it Ibrāhīm?' Ibrāhīm said, "By him, Allah's proof was established over the worshippers of idols and stars."

قِيلَ: هُوَ مُوسَى ، قَالَ: مُوسَى أَخُوهُ وَلَكِنْ:

هَذَا حَبِيبٌ وَمُوسَى كَلِيمٌ وَمُخَاطِب ۝

It was asked, 'Is it Mūsā?' He said, "Mūsā is his brother, this is Ḥabīb (the beloved) and Mūsā is Kalīm and Mukhāṭab," (the speech and the addressee).

[38] This is the scene of a conversation between the angelic realm, the Prophets and Allah, regarding the mystery of this light that Allah had created. There is no specific reference to the authenticity of this conversation in this context and wording.

قِيْلَ: هُوَ عِيْسَى، قَـالَ: عِيْسَى

يُبَشِّرُ بِهِ وَهُوَ بَيْنَ يَدَىْ نُبُوَّتِهِ كَالْحَاجِبِ ۝

It was asked, 'Is it ʿĪsā?' ʿĪsā said, "By him, there were glad tidings and he was like a veil before his Prophethood."

قِيْلَ: فَمَنْ هَذَا الْحَبِيْبُ الْكَرِيْمُ الَّذِي أَلْبَسْتَهُ حُلَّةَ الْوَقَارِ،

It was asked, "So who is this noble beloved, whom You clothed with intimacy and reverence, enthroned

وَتَوَّجْتَهُ بِتِيْجَانِ الْمَهَابَةِ وَالْإِفْتِخَارِ ۝

وَنَشَرْتَ عَلَى رَأْسِهِ الْعَصَائِبَ ۝

with the crown of dignity and glory,
and sent troops before him.

قَالَ: هُوَ نَبِيٌّ إِسْتَخَرْتُهُ مِنْ لُؤَيِّ بْنِ غَالِبٍ ۝ يَمُوْتُ أَبُوْهُ

وَأُمُّهُ وَثَمَّ عَمُّهُ الشَّقِيْقُ أَبُوْ طَالِبٍ ۝

Allah said, "He is a Prophet, and I have selected him from Luʿay ibn Ghālib. His father and mother will pass away, and his uncle, Abū Ṭālib will support him.

اللّٰهُمَّ صَلِّ وَسَلِّمْ وَبَارِكْ عَلَيْهِ

O Allah send peace and blessings upon him

يُبْعَثُ مِنْ تِهَامَةْ ۞ بَيْنَ يَدَيِ الْقِيَامَةْ ۞

فِي ظَهْرِهِ عَلَامَةْ ۞ تُظِلُّهُ الْغَمَامَهْ ۞

He will be sent from Tihāma after him will be the Day of Judgement.[39]
Upon his back will be a sign,[40] he will be shaded by the clouds,[41]

تُطِيعُهُ السَّحَائِبْ ۞ فَجْرِيُّ الْجَبِينِ لَيْلِيُّ الذَّوَائِبْ ۞

أَلْفِيُّ الْأَنْفِ نُونِيُّ الْحَاجِبْ ۞

And they will comply to him.[42] He will have a forehead, with radiance of the dawn;[43] locks of hair like the night,[a] an aquiline nose and arched eyebrows.[b]

---

[39] This is derived from his saying ﷺ "I was sent and the Hour like these two," [indicating with his two fingers]. Narrated in Bukhārī and Muslim. Another version states, "I was sent and with me the Day of Judgement." Related by Aḥmad and others.

[40] This refers to the seal of Prophethood, which is mentioned in the *Ṣaḥīḥ*.

[41] The clouds shaded him, in order to be protected from the heat of sun. It has been related that the clouds would shade him ﷺ this was seen in his journey to *Shām,* with his uncle and it was one of the signs of Prophethood in his early years. Tirmīdhī, Ḥakīm, Bayhaqī, Ibn Asākir and Ibn Kathīr have cited it.

[42] The clouds would respond to him with the falling of rain, this is affirmed in the *Ṣaḥīḥ* that he ﷺ asked for rain, so the clouds gathered [to the extent that] not a part of the sky was visible. Then he indicated with his hand, whereupon, the clouds dispersed and the sky became clear just as it was before.

[43] His forehead radiated like the light of dawn, as stated in the Ḥadīth: "It was as though the sun was rising upon his face ﷺ. Cited by Ibn Saᶜd and Tirmīdhi. It has also been related, "His face was like a phase of the moon." Narrated in Bukhārī.

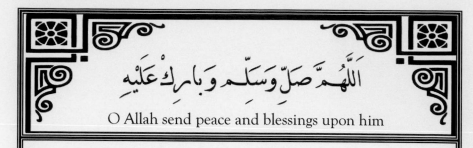

سَمْعُهُ يَسْمَعُ صَرِيرَ الْقَلَمِ بَصَرُهُ إِلَى السَّبْعِ الطِّبَاقِ ثَاقِبٍ ۝

قَدَمَاهُ قَبَّلَهُمَا الْبَعِيرُ فَازَالَ مَا اشْتَكَاهُ مِنَ الْمِحَنِ وَالنَّوَائِبِ ۝

His hearing will hear the scribing of the Pen and his sight will pierce through the seven heavens.[44] The camel kissed his feet, [45] which removed her complaint of trial and hardships.

آمَنَ بِهِ الضَّبُّ وَسَلَّمَتْ عَلَيْهِ الْأَشْجَارُ

وَخَاطَبَتْهُ الْأَحْجَارُ وَحَنَّ إِلَيْهِ الْجِذْعُ حَنِينَ حَزِينٍ نَادِبٍ ۝

The lizard believed in him[46] and the trees greeted him.[47] The stones addressed him,[48] and the sad, weeping tree trunk yearned for him.[49]

---

[a] The expression of night here refers to the shade of ebony.

[b] There is a connotation of beauty with the letters of the Arabic alphabet due to the lucid shapes that they hold. The letters are expressions, often used in poetry to heighten the beauty of facial features, with regards to their distinct shapes. Here we have *alīf* to describe the aquilinity of the nose, the head of the *mīm,* which describes the perfect curve of the lips and the curvature of the *nūn* that describes the brow.

[44] His hearing the scribing of the Pen refers to the event of the ascension (*miʿrāj*) in a sound Ḥadīth. Moreover, regarding the acuteness of sight and sound there is reference in the Sunan of Tirmīdhī and Ibn Māja: "The Messenger of Allah ﷺ said, "I see what you do not and I hear that which you do not hear." There are many Ḥadīths in the *Ṣaḥīḥ* that allude to the acuteness of his sight, which was inconceivable like his ability to see from behind as in front, his ability to see heaven, the hellfire, the realm of the angels. And likewise his hearing, wherewith he heard the sound of the stones being cast in the hellfire. Related in *Ṣaḥīḥ* Muslim.

[45] Many Ḥadīths have been related on the camel, and cited by Aḥmad, Ibn Abī Shayba, Bazzār, Abū Nuʿaym, Dārmī, Bayhaqī and Ṭabrānī. Some of the following: "The camel fell down in prostration", "It came with its lips against the earth until it knelt down before him." And mentioned in the Ḥadīth of Aḥmad that the Companions, (may Allah be pleased with them all) said: "O Messenger of Allah, this animal has no intellect yet it prostrates to you, it is more fitting that we prostrate to you." He replied, " It is not appropriate for a man to prostrate to a man." Cited by Ibn Kathīr with an excellent chain of transmission.

[46] The Ḥadīth of the lizard's faith was related by (*Sayyidinā*) ʿUmar ibn al-Khaṭṭāb and has been cited by Ṭabarānī in his '*Awṣat*', by Ḥakim in his '*Mujʿizāt*' by Ibn

يَدَاهُ تَظْهَرُ بَرَكَتُهُمَا فِي الْمَطَاعِمِ وَالْمَشَارِب ۝

قَلْبُهُ لَا يَغْفُلُ وَلَا يَنَامُ وَلَكِنْ لِلْخِدْمَةِ عَلَى الدَّوَامِ مُرَاقِب ۝

His hands will manifest their blessings in food and drink.[50]
His heart will not be heedless, nor will it sleep,[51] but to serve; it will always be observant.

إِنْ أُوذِيَ يَعْفُ وَلَا يُعَاقِب ۝ وَإِنْ خُوصِمَ يَصْمُتْ وَلَا يُجَاوِب

أَرْفَعُهُ إِلَى أَشْرَفِ الْمَرَاتِب ۝

If he is harmed, he will forgive and will not punish.[52] And if he is provoked, he will remain silent and will not respond. I will raise him to the noblest station,

---

ᶜAdiy, Bayhaqī, Abū Naᶜīm, Ibn Asākir and Suyūtī in his *'Khasā'is'* vol.2, p. 276, however, Ibn Kathīr says that it is disputed and unknown.

[47] The greeting of the trees is mentioned in a Ḥadīth on the authority of (*Sayyidinā*) ᶜUmar ibn al-Khaṭṭāb, which has been cited by Ibn Saᶜd, Abū Yaᶜlā, Bazzār, Bayhaqī and Abū Naᶜīm with a sound transmission. And it has been mentioned on the authority of (*Sayyidinā*) ᶜAlī, who said, "We were with the Messenger of Allah, ﷺ in Makkah, he went in some directions, there was not a tree, nor a mountain that greeted him but that it said, 'Peace be upon you O Messenger of Allah.'" Related by Dārmī and Tirmīdhī.

[48] The speaking of the stones is in reference to a Ḥadīth as follows: "I know of every stone in Makkah that greets me". Cited in *Ṣaḥīḥ* Muslim and by others.

[49] The Ḥadīth of the weeping tree trunk has been mentioned in the *Ṣaḥīḥ* through many chains of transmissions.

[50] It has been mentioned in Bukhārī and Muslim, through many sound transmissions that water emanated from his fingers ﷺ. Furthermore, there is mention, therein, of a large number that quenched their thirst from the blessings of his palms.

[51] Mentioned in a Ḥadīth that (*Sayyida*) ᶜĀ'isha (رضي الله عنها) said: "O Messenger of Allah, Do you sleep before you perform your *wiṭr*?" He replied, "O ᶜĀ'isha, my eyes sleep, but my heart does not sleep." Narrated by Bukhārī in his *Ṣaḥīḥ* in the 'Book of *Tahajjud*'.

[52] It has been mentioned in a sound Ḥadīth on the authority of *Sayyida* ᶜĀ'isha (رضي الله عنها) who said that: "The Prophet ﷺ was not offensive." And she said, "He did not respond to evil with evil, but he forgave and overlooked."

فِي رَكْبَةٍ لَاتَنْبَغِي قَبْلَهُ وَلَابَعْدَهُ لِرَاكِب ○

فِي مَوْكِبٍ مِنَ الْمَلَائِكَةِ يَفُوقُ عَلَى سَائِرِ الْمَوَاكِب ○

In a carriage that no one has travelled, before him nor after him,
in a procession of angels that will surpass all processions.

فَإِذَا ارْتَقَى عَلَى الْكَوْنَيْنِ وَانْفَصَلَ عَنِ الْعَالَمِينَ ○

وَوَصَلَ إِلَى قَابَ قَوْسَيْنِ كُنْتُ لَهُ أَنَا النَّدِيمُ وَالْمُخَاطِبُ ○

Thus he ascended both universes, separated from all realms, and arrived at two bows length.
[The Exalted said] "I am for him, I am the Intimate and the Addresser." [53]

[53] This refers to the description of the miraculous night journey and the ascension. The procession refers to the escorts, servants and entourage of splendour and beauty, the likes of which no prophet or angel, neither before him nor after him has ever acquired.

اَللّٰهُمَّ صَلِّ وَسَلِّمْ وَبَارِكْ عَلَيْهِ

O' Allah send peace and blessings upon him

ثُمَّ أَرُدُّهُ مِنَ الْعَرْشِ ۝ قَبْلَ أَنْ يَبْرُدَ الْفَرْشُ ۝

وَقَدْ نَالَ جَمِيعَ الْمَآرِبْ ۝

"Then, I shall return him from the Throne before the earth freezes."
And all his wishes were fulfilled.

فَإِذَا شُرِّفَتْ تُرْبَةُ طَيِّبَةَ مِنْهُ بِأَشْرَفِ قَالَبْ ۝

سَعَتْ إِلَيْهِ أَرْوَاحُ الْمُحِبِّينَ عَلَى الْأَقْدَامِ وَالنَّجَائِبْ ۝

The earth was honoured with the noblest of forms.
The spirits of the lovers and the noble ones ran towards him on their feet.

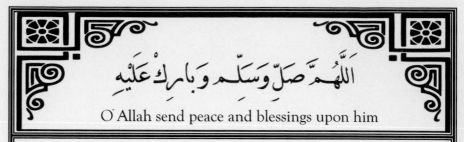

صَلَاةُ اللهِ مَا دَارَتْ كَوَاكِبْ

عَلَى أَحْمَدَ خَيْرِ مَنْ رَكِبَ النَّجَائِبْ

May the blessings of Allah be upon Ahmad,[c]
the best of the Nobles that rode, as long as the planets rotate.

حَدَا حَادِي السُّرَى بِاسْمِ الْحَبَائِبْ

فَهَزَّ السُّكْرُ أَعْطَافَ الرَّكَائِبْ

The cameleer urged the camel in the name of the beloved,
the intoxication moved the camels with joy.

[c] This section is the *raḥīl of the qasīda,* i.e. the part of the poem that describes the venture through the desert in order to meet the beloved. And thus, this is the poet's description of the journey to Madīna, the city of the Prophet.

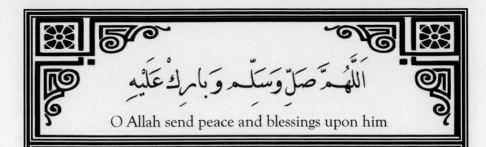

أَلَمْ تَــرَهَا وَقَــدْ مَــدَّتْ خُطَاهَا

وَسَــالَتْ مِــنْ مَدَامِعِهَا سَحَائِبْ

Did you not see her as she extended her strides?
and clouds formed from the flow of her tears.

فَدَعْ جَذْبَ الزِّمَامِ وَلَا تَسُــقْهَا

فَــقَائِدُ شَوْقِهَا لِلْحَيِّ جَــاذِبْ

Cease pulling the reigns, and do not drive her,
As the one who incites her desire for Allah, is pulling

فَــهِمْ طَرَباً كَمَا هَــامَتْ وَإِلَّا

فَــإِنَّكَ فِي طَــرِيْقِ الْحُبِّ كَاذِبْ

Then, endeavor delightfully just as she endeavors,
or else you are a liar on the path of love.

أَمَــا هَــذَا الْعَقِيْقُ بَدَا وَهَذِي

قِــبَابُ الْحَيِّ لَاحَتْ وَالْمَضَارِبْ

Truly this ravine has appeared; and these domes
Of life and camps have illuminated.

وَتِـــلْكَ القُبَّةُ الْخَضْرَاءُ فِيْهَا

نَبِيٌّ نُـوْرُهُ يَجْــلُو الْغَــيَاهِبُ

That is the green dome, wherein a prophet lies,
whose light illuminates the darkness.

وَقَــدْ صَحَّ الرِّضَا وَدَنَا التَّـلاَقِي

وَقَــدْ جَاءَ الْهَنَا مِـنْ كُلِّ جَانِبْ

Pleasure has been fulfilled; radiance has drawn near,
and merriment advanced from every direction

فَقُـــلْ لِلنَّفْسِ دُونَـــكَ وَالتَّمَلِّي

فَمَا دُونَ الْحَـــبِيْبِ الْيَوْمَ حَاجِبْ

Say to the soul, 'Here you are, enjoy
for there is no barrier in front of the beloved.'

تَمَـــلَّى بِالْحَـــبِيْبِ بِكُلِّ قَصْدٍ

فَقَــدْ حَصَــلَ الْهَنَا وَالضِّدُّ غَائِبْ

Enjoy the beloved, with every intention.
Felicity has come to pass and its opposite is absent.

نَبِيُّ اللهِ خَيْرُ الْخَلْقِ جَمْعاً

لَهُ أَعْلَى الْمَنَاصِبِ وَالْمَرَاتِبِ

The Prophet of Allah, the best of all creation,
Who has the highest station and rank.

لَهُ الْجَاهُ الرَّفِيعُ لَهُ الْمَعَالِي

لَهُ الشَّرَفُ الْمُؤَبَّدُ وَالْمَنَاقِبِ

He has an exalted standing, he has excellence,
perpetual honour and virtues.

فَلَوْ أَنَّا سَعَيْنَا كُلَّ حِينٍ

عَلَى الْأَحْدَاقِ لَا فَوْقَ النَّجَائِبِ

If only we had strived at all times for [his] glances,
we would have surpassed the nobles.

وَلَوْ أَنَّا عَمِلْنَا كُلَّ يَوْمِ

لِأَحْمَدَ مَوْلِدًا قَدْ كَانَ وَاجِبِ

And if we held a mawlid everyday,
For Ahmad it would be an obligation,

عَلَيْهِ مِنَ الْمُهَيْمِنِ كُلَّ وَقْتٍ

صَلاَةٌ مَا بَدَا نُورُ الْكَوَاكِبِ

May there be a blessing upon him, throughout time,
from Allah, as long as the light of the planets illuminate.

تَعُمَّ الآلَ وَالأَصْحَابَ طُرًّا

جَمِيعَهُمُ وَعِتْرَتَهُ الاَطَايِبْ

May it include all the family, the Companions,
And his pure descendents

فَسُبْحَانَ مَنْ خَصَّهُ صَلَّى اللهُ عَلَيْهِ وَسَلَّمَ

بِأَشْرَافِ الْمَنَاصِبِ وَالْمَرَاتِبِ ۝

And glory be to the One Who distinguished him ﷺ
with the noblest of ranks and stations.

أَحْمَدُهُ عَلَى مَا مَنَحَ مِنَ الْمَوَاهِبِ ۝ وَأَشْهَدُ أَنْ لَآ إِلٰهَ إِلَّا اللهُ

وَحْدَهُ لَا شَرِيكَ لَهُ رَبُّ الْمَشَارِقِ وَالْمَغَارِب ۝

I praise Him (Allah) for the gifts that He has bestowed and testify that there is no God but Allah alone, without partner, the Lord of the Easts and the Wests.

وَأَشْهَدُ أَنَّ سَيِّدَنَا مُحَمَّدًا عَبْدُهُ وَرَسُولُهُ

الْمَبْعُوثُ إِلَى سَائِرِ الْأَعَاجِمِ وَالْأَعَارِبِ ۝

And, I testify that Sayyidinā Muhammad is His servant and Messenger,
sent to all, the non-Arabs and the Arabs.

صَلَّى اللهُ عَلَيْهِ وَعَلَى آلِهِ

وَأَصْحَابِهِ أُولِي الْمَآثِرِ وَالْمَنَاقِبِ ۝

May the peace and blessings of Allah be upon him, his family
and his Companions the people of victory and virtue.

صَلَاةً وَسَلَامًا دَائِمَيْنِ مُتَلَازِمَيْنِ

يَأْتِي قَائِلُهُمَا يَوْمَ الْقِيَامَةِ غَيْرَ خَائِبْ ۝

The one who invokes everlasting peace and blessings [upon him] will be successful on the Day of Rising.

اللَّهُمَّ صَلِّ وَسَلِّمْ وَبَارِكْ عَلَيْهِ

O Allah send peace and blessings upon him

بِسْمِ اللَّهِ الرَّحْمَٰنِ الرَّحِيمِ

أَوَّلُ مَا نَسْتَفْتِحُ بِإِيرَادِ حَدِيثَيْنِ وَرَدَا عَنْ نَبِيِّ

كَانَ قَدْرُهُ عَظِيمًا ۝ وَنَسَبُهُ كَرِيمًا ۝ وَصِرَاطُهُ مُسْتَقِيمًا ۝

First, we will commence by citing two Ḥadīths, related on the authority of the Prophet whose prestige is exalted, lineage most noble and whose path is straight.

قَالَ فِي حَقِّهِ مَنْ لَمْ يَزَلْ سَمِيعًا عَلِيمًا :

He (the Exalted), Who is always Hearing, Knowing said, with respect to him:

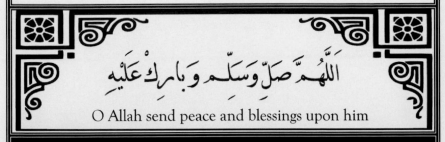

﴿إِنَّ اللهَ وَمَلَائِكَتَهُ يُصَلُّونَ عَلَى النَّبِيِّ

يَا أَيُّهَا الَّذِينَ آمَنُوا صَلُّوا عَلَيْهِ وَسَلِّمُوا تَسْلِيمًا﴾

"Indeed Allah and His angels shower blessings upon the Prophet. O you who believe, invoke blessings on him and salute him with a worthy salutation."

اَللَّهُمَّ صَلِّ وَسَلِّمْ وَبَارِكْ عَلَيْهِ

O Allah send peace and blessings upon him

(اَلْحَدِيثُ الأَوَّلُ):

عَنْ بَحْرِ الْعِلْمِ الدَّافِقِ ۝ وَلِسَانِ الْقُرْآنِ النَّاطِقِ ۝

أَوْحَدِ عُلَمَاءِ النَّاسِ ۝

The first Ḥadīth is on the authority of the enlightened one, who spoke by the words of the Qur'ān the most distinguished scholar of the people,

سَيِّدِنَا عَبْدَ اللهِ بْنِ سَيِّدِنَا الْعَبَّاسِ رَضِيَ اللهُ عَنْهُمَا

عَنْ رَسُولِ اللهِ صَلَّى اللهُ عَلَيْهِ وَسَلَّمَ أَنَّهُ قَالَ:

Sayyidinā ᶜAbdallāh ibn Sayyidinā al-ᶜAbbās ﵄, he related from the Messenger of Allah ﷺ the following:

كُنتُ نُوراً بَيْنَ يَدَيِ اللهِ عَزَّ وَجَلَّ قَبْلَ أَنْ يَخْلُقَ آدَمَ

بِأَلْفَيْ عَامٍ يُسَبِّحُ اللهَ ذَلِكَ النُّورُ وَتُسَبِّحُ الْمَلَائِكَةُ بِتَسْبِيحِهِ ۝

"I was a light in the presence of Allah Mighty and Majestic is He,[54] two thousand years before He created Adam. This light was glorifying Allah, and the angels were glorifying (Him) with this glorification.

فَلَمَّا خَلَقَ اللهُ آدَمَ أَلْقَى ذَلِكَ النُّورَ فِي طِينَتِهِ قَالَ صَلَّى اللهُ

عَلَيْهِ وَسَلَّمَ: فَأَهْبَطَنِي اللهُ عَزَّ وَجَلَّ إِلَى الأَرْضِ فِي ظَهْرِ آدَمَ ۝

When Allah created Adam, that light was cast into his clay.
He ﷺ said, Then Allah descended me to the earth in the spine of Adam,

وَحَمَلَنِي فِي السَّفِينَةِ فِي صُلْبِ نُوحٍ ۝

وَجَعَلَنِي فِي صُلْبِ الْخَلِيلِ إِبْرَاهِيمَ حِينَ قُذِفَ بِهِ فِي النَّارِ ۝

And He carried me in the ark, in the loins of Nūḥ.
Then, He placed me in the loins of the Friend, Ibrāhīm, when he was cast into the fire.

[54] Muḥammad ibn ᶜUmar al-ᶜAdnī, Ibn al-Jawzi in his *'Wafa'*, Suyūṭī in his *'Masnūᶜāt'* and Qādī ᶜIyād in his *'Al-Shifā"* have mentioned this and said that the famous poem of Ibn ᶜAbbās in praise of the Prophet ﷺ verifies the authenticity of this Ḥadīth. Al-Ḥāfiẓ ibn ᶜAbd al-Barr has quoted these verses in his work on Kharīm ibn Aws who said, 'I migrated to the Messenger of Allah ﷺ I went towards him as he was leaving Tabūk and I heard his uncle ᶜAbbās say: "O Messenger of Allah, I want to praise you." The Prophet ﷺ said, "Say, how well Allah has made you say!" Then he related his poetry…" Ibn ᶜAbbās ﷺ has related in his commentary of v. 219 in *Ṣūrat al-Shuᶜarā': "And your movement among those who fall prostrate"* an interpretation that supports the emergence of the Prophet. He said that he turned in the loins of the prophets until his mother gave birth to him. Related by Ibn Abī Ḥātim, Ibn Mardawiyya and Abū Naᶜīm in his *'Dalā'il'*. This has also been mentioned in the *tafsīr* of Ibn Kathīr, Ibn Abī Ḥātim and Ibn al-Jawzī.

وَلَمْ يَزَلِ اللهُ عَزَّ وَجَلَّ يَنْقُلُنِي مِنَ الأَصْلَابِ الطَّاهِرَةِ

إِلَى الأَرْحَامِ الزَّكِيَّةِ الْفَاخِرَةِ ۝

Allah Mighty and Majestic is He, continued to carry me through pure loins, into the pure and glorious wombs,

حَتَّى أَخْرَجَنِي اللهُ مِنْ بَيْنِ أَبَوَيَّ وَهُمَا لَمْ يَلْتَقِيَا عَلَى سِفَاحٍ قَطُّ

Until Allah emitted me through my parents, who never met by fornication."[55]

---

[55] It has been related on the authority of Abū Huraira that the Messenger of Allah ﷺ said: "I was sent through the best generations of the children of Adam, generation after generation until I was sent to the generation that I am in." Narrated in Bukhārī. In *Ṣaḥīḥ* Muslim it has been narrated on the authority of Wāthila ibn al-Asqā' that the Messenger of Allah ﷺ said: "Allah chose Banī Kināna from the children of Ismāᶜīl, and He chose the Qureish from Banī Kināna, and He chose Banī Ḥāshim from the Qureish, and He chose me from the Banī Ḥāshim." Imām Aḥmad has related on the authority of Ibn ᶜAbbās that the Messenger of Allah ﷺ said: "I am Muhammad the son of ᶜAbdallāh, the son of ᶜAbd al-Mutalib, Allah created the creation and He made me the best of His creation. He divided them into two groups and placed me in the best group. He created tribes and placed me in the best tribe, and He made them into families and placed me in the best family, so of your families my family is the best, and I am the best amongst you." Through many transmissions it has been affirmed that he ﷺ said: "I emerged through wedlock and not through adultery." In another version: "I was not born from any adultery of *Jāhiliyya*, I was only born through wedlock like the wedlock of Islam." Another version states: "I only emerged through purity." Related by Ibn Saᶜd, Ibn Asākir, Ṭabarānī, Ibn Abī Shayba, Suyūtī has mentioned it in his '*Khasā'is*' and Ibn Kathīr has mentioned it in his '*Bidāya*'. In the narration of Abū Naᶜīm: "My parents never met by adultery; Allah continued to move me from pure loins to pure wombs, pure and refined. Two groups did not emerge only that I was in the best of them." Narrated by Ṭabrānī in his '*Awsat*' and by Bayhaqī in his '*Dalā'il*' on the authority of (*Sayyida*) ᶜĀ'isha ﷺ that the Messenger of Allah ﷺ said: "Jibrīl said to me, "I roamed around the earth in its East and its West, and I did not find a man better than Muhammad and I did not find a tribe better than Banī Ḥāshim."" Related by Suyūṭī and Ḥāfiẓ Ibn Ḥajar.

اَللّٰهُمَّ صَلِّ وَسَلِّمْ وَبَارِكْ عَلَيْهِ

O Allah send peace and blessings upon him

(الحَدِيثُ الثَّانِي)

عَنْ عَطَاءِ بْنِ يَسَارٍ عَنْ كَعْبِ الْأَحْبَارِ قَالَ: عَلَّمَنِي أَبِي

التَّوْرَاةَ إِلَّا سِفْرًا وَاحِدًا كَانَ يَخْتِمُهُ وَيُدْخِلُهُ الصُّنْدُوقَ

The second Ḥadīth is cited on the authority of ʿAṭā' ibn Yasār ﵁, who related it in on the authority of Kaʿb al-Aḥbār ﵁ who said:
"My father taught me the Torah, except for one book, whereupon, he would stop and place it back into the case.

فَلَمَّا مَاتَ أَبِي فَتَحْتُهُ فَإِذَا فِيهِ: نَبِيٌّ يَخْرُجُ آخِرَ الزَّمَانِ ۝

مَوْلِدُهُ بِمَكَّةَ، وَهِجْرَتُهُ بِالْمَدِينَةِ، وَسُلْطَانُهُ بِالشَّام

When my father passed away, I opened it and lo, therein [was mention of] a Prophet, who will emerge at the end of time.
His birth will be in Makkah, his migration will be to Madina, and his dominion, will be in Shām.

يَقُصُّ شَعْرَهُ، وَيَتَّزِرُ عَلَى وَسَطِهِ ۝ يَكُونُ خَيْرَ الْأَنْبِيَاءِ،

وَأُمَّتُهُ خَيْرَ الْأُمَمِ ۝ يُكَبِّرُونَ اللهَ تَعَالَى عَلَى كُلِّ شَرَفٍ ۝

His hair will be cut and he will wrap a cloth around his waist. He will be the best of Prophets; his ummah will be the best of communities and they will extol Allah the Exalted with great honour.

يَصُفُّونَ فِي الصَّلاَةِ كَصُفُوفِهِمْ فِي الْقِتَالِ ۝

قُلُوبُهُمْ مَصَاحِفُهُمْ يَحْمَدُونَ اللهَ تَعَالَى عَلَى كُلِّ شِدَّةٍ وَرَخَاءٍ ۝

Their aligning for prayer will be like their alignments in battle.
Their hearts will [bear] their scriptures and they will praise Allah the Exalted, in every hardship and ease.

ثُلُثٌ يَدْخُلُونَ الْجَنَّةَ بِغَيْرِ حِسَابٍ ۝

وَثُلُثٌ يَأْتُونَ بِذُنُوبِهِمْ وَخَطَايَاهُمْ فَيُغْفَرُ لَهُمْ ۝

A third of them will enter heaven without reckoning, a third will come forth with their sins and faults and they will be forgiven.[56]

وَثُلُثٌ يَأْتُونَ بِذُنُوبٍ وَخَطَايَا عِظَامٍ ۝

فَيَقُولُ اللهُ تَعَالَى لِلْمَلاَئِكَةِ: اِذْهَبُوا فَزِنُوهُمْ ،

A third will come forth with sins and great faults.
Then, Allah the Exalted will say to the Angels, "Go and weigh them."

---

[56] The statement of the Exalted verifies this Ḥadīth: "*Then We made our chosen slaves inherit the Book. But some of them wrong themselves, some are ambivalent, and some outdo eachother in good by Allah's permission,that is the great favour*" Qur'ān [35:32]. Likewise the Ḥadīth related by Ibn Abī Ḥātim: Muhammad ibn ᶜAzīz related, Salama related on the authority of ᶜAqīl, on the authority of Shihāb on the authority of ᶜAwf ibn Mālik, may Allah be pleased with him that the Messenger of Allah, may blessings and peace be upon him said: "My *ummah* is divided into three, a third will enter the Garden without reckoning or torment, a third will be reckoned with an easy reckoning then they will enter the Garden, and a third will be purified and relieved. Then the angels will come and say, "We found them saying 'There is no God but Allah alone. Then Allah the Exalted will say: 'You are truthful that there is no God but I, enter them on account of their statement 'There is no God but Allah alone,' and take their sins to the people of the Fire." This refers to Allah's statement: "*They will bear their own burdens and other burdens together with their own.*" Qur'ān [29:13]

فَيَقُولُونَ: يَا رَبَّنَا وَجَدْنَاهُمْ أَسْرَفُوا عَلَى أَنْفُسِهِمْ،

وَوَجَدْنَا أَعْمَالَهُمْ مِنَ الذُّنُوبِ كَأَمْثَالِ الْجِبَالِ،

They will say, "O our Lord we found that they have wronged themselves, and we found that their deeds of sins are like mountains,

غَيْرَ أَنَّهُمْ يَشْهَدُونَ أَنْ لَا إِلَهَ إِلَّا اللهُ وَأَنَّ مُحَمَّدًا رَسُولُ اللهِ

صَلَّى اللهُ عَلَيْهِ وَسَلَّمَ ۝ فَيَقُولُ الْحَقُّ: وَعِزَّتِي وَجَلَالِي

however, they have testified that there is no god but Allah and that Muhammad is the Messenger of Allah ﷺ." Then, Allah will say, "By My Honour and My Majesty,

لَا جَعَلْتُ مَنْ أَخْلَصَ لِي بِالشَّهَادَةِ

كَمَنْ كَذَّبَ بِي، أَدْخِلُوهُمُ الْجَنَّةَ بِرَحْمَتِي ۝

I have not likened the one sincere to Me in the Testification like the one who denies Me; enter them into heaven by My Mercy."

اللّٰهُمَّ صَلِّ وَسَلِّمْ وَبَارِكْ عَلَيْهِ

O Allah send peace and blessings upon him

يَا أَعَزَّ جَوَاهِرِ الْعُقُودِ، وَخُلَاصَةَ إِكْسِيرِ سِرِّ الْوُجُودِ،

مَادِحُكَ قَاصِرٌ وَلَوْ جَاءَ بِبَذْلِ الْمَجْهُودِ،

O The Greatest Essence, O the Quintessence of existence, the one who praises You is incapable [of praising You], even if he exerts himself with all endeavour.

وَوَاصِفُكَ عَاجِزٌ عَنْ حَصْرِ مَا حَوَيْتَ مِنْ خِصَالِ الْكَرَمِ

وَالْجُودِ الْكَوْنُ، إِشَارَةٌ وَأَنْتَ الْمَقْصُودُ ۝

And your admirer is unable to enumerate the noble and generous attributes that You possess. The universe is a sign and You are the Goal.

يَا أَشْرَفَ مَنْ نَالَ الْمَقَامَ الْمَحْمُودَ، وَجَاءَتْ رُسُلٌ

مِنْ قَبْلِكَ لَـٰكِنَّهُمْ بِالرِّفْعَةِ وَالْعُلَى لَكَ شُهُودٌ ۝

O the most noble, the one who received the praiseworthy station messengers came before you, but they were only witnesses to your sublime stature and eminence.

اَللَّهُمَّ صَلِّ وَسَلِّمْ وَبَارِكْ عَلَيْهِ

O Allah send peace and blessings upon him

أَحْضِرُوا قُلُوبَكُمْ يَا مَعْشَرَ ذَوِي الْأَلْبَابْ، حَتَّى أَجْلُوَ لَكُمْ

عَرَائِسَ مَعَانِي أَجَلِّ الْأَحْبَابْ ۞

Make present your hearts, O People of understanding, so that the significance of the most eminent beloved will be revealed to you.

اَلْمَخْصُوصِ بِأَشْرَفِ الْأَلْقَابْ ۞ اَلرَّاقِي إِلَى حَضْرَةِ الْمَلِكِ

الْوَهَّابْ ۞ حَتَّى نَظَرَ إِلَى جَمَالِهِ بِلَا سِتْرٍ وَلَا حِجَابْ ۞

He who has been distinguished with the noblest title. He ascended to the presence of the Most Benevolent King, until he saw His Beauty without cover or veil.

فَلَمَّا آنَ أَوَانُ ظُهُورِ شَمْسِ الرِّسَالَةِ فِي سَمَاءِ الْجَلَالَةْ خَرَجَ

مَرْسُومُ الْجَلِيلْ ۞ لِنَقِيبِ الْمَمْلَكَةِ جِبْرِيلْ ۞

When the rays of the Message emerged in the majestic heaven, the divine ordinance was dispatched to the chief of the angels, Jibrīl.

يَا جِبْرِيلُ نَادِ فِي سَائِرِ الْمَخْلُوقَاتِ ۝ مِنْ أَهْلِ الْأَرْضِ وَ

السَّمَاوَاتِ ۝ بِالتَّهَانِي وَالْبِشَارَاتِ ۝

"O Jibrīl, proclaim the glad tidings and good news to all of creation,in the earth and the heavens, with congratulations and glad tidings,

فَإِنَّ النُّورَ الْمَصُونَ ۝ وَالسِّرَّ الْمَكْنُونَ ۝ الَّذِي أَوْجَدْتُهُ

قَبْلَ وُجُودِ الْأَشْيَاءِ ۝ وَإِبْدَاعِ الْأَرْضِ وَالسَّمَاءِ ۝

that the protected light, the concealed secret,created before all things, before the heavens and the earth;

أَنْقُلُهُ فِي هَذِهِ اللَّيْلَةِ إِلَى بَطْنِ أُمِّهِ مَسْرُورًا ۝ أَمْلَأُ بِهِ

الْكَوْنَ نُورًا أَكْفُلُهُ يَتِيمًا ۝ وَأُطَهِّرُهُ وَأَهْلَ بَيْتِهِ تَطْهِيرًا ۝

in this night I will transmit, to the womb of his delighted mother.[57] I will protect him as an orphan, and I will greatly purify him and his family.

[57] This has been mentioned in '*al-Mawāhib*' Vol. 1, p. 19, on the authority of Khatīb Baghdādī, on the authority of Sahl ibn ᶜAbdallāh al-Tusṭarī and a similar version has been mentioned on the authority of Kaᶜb al-Aḥbār. However, I did not find that the chain of transmitters went back to the Prophet ﷺ.

اَللّٰهُمَّ صَلِّ وَسَلِّمْ وَبَارِكْ عَلَيْهِ

O Allah send peace and blessings upon him

فَاهْتَزَّ الْعَرْشُ طَرَبًا وَّاسْتِبْشَارًا ۝ وَازْدَادَ الْكُرْسِيُّ

هَيْبَةً وَّوَقَارًا ۝ وَامْتَلَأَتِ السَّمَاوَاتُ أَنْوَارًا ۝

The Throne (*ᶜArsh*) shook with delight and happiness, the Footstool (*Kursī*) increased in its magnanimity and reverence, and the heavens were filled with light.

وَضَجَّتِ الْمَلَائِكَةُ تَهْلِيلًا وَتَمْجِيدًا وَاسْتِغْفَارًا ۝

وَلَمْ تَزَلْ أُمُّهُ تَرَى أَنْوَاعًا مِنْ فَخْرِهِ وَفَضْلِهِ ۝

The angels cried the praises of *tahlīl, tamjīd* and *istighfār*.[A]
His mother constantly witnessed many of his glories and blessings, until the end of her pregnancy.

[A] Recite *'SubḥānalLāh wa'l-ḤamdulilLāh, wa Lā ilāha illalLāh, wa'lLāhu Akbar'* four times.

إِلَى نِهَايَةِ تَمَامِ حَمْلِهِ ۞ فَلَمَّا اشْتَدَّ بِهَا الطَّلْقُ بِإِذْنِ رَبِّ

الْخَلْقِ وَضَعَتِ الْحَبِيبَ صَلَّى اللهُ عَلَيْهِ وَسَلَّمَ ،

سَاجِدًا شَاكِرًا حَامِدًا كَأَنَّهُ الْبَدْرُ فِي تَمَامِهِ ۞

(هنا محل القيام)

When the labour became intense, by the permission of the Lord of creation, she gave birth to al-Ḥabīb ﷺ who was prostrating, thankful, and praising;[58] he resembled the full moon. [Qiyam]

---

[58] There is a Ḥadīth in 'Al-Mawāhib' on the authority of Ibn ʿAbbās that (Sayyida) Āmina ؆ gave birth to him, then she looked at him and found him prostrating and he raised his fingers to the sky like the entreating supplicant." Related by Abu Naʿīm and a similar version by Ṭabarānī.

[Qiyam] This is the place of standing in honour and reverence of the Prophet's birth ﷺ.
Turn to page 88.

اَللّٰهُمَّ صَلِّ وَسَلِّمْ وَبَارِكْ عَلَيْهِ

O Allah send peace and blessings upon him

وَوُلِدَ صَلَّى اللّٰهُ عَلَيْهِ وَسَلَّمَ مَخْتُوْنًا بِيَدِ الْعِنَايَهْ ۝

مَكْحُوْلًا بِكُحْلِ الْهِدَايَهْ ۝ فَأَشْرَقَ بِبَهَائِهِ الْفَضَا ۝

He ﷺ was born circumcised [59] under the shade of protection and anointed with the kohl of guidance. The cosmos radiated with his splendor,

وَتَلَأْلَأَ الْكَوْنُ مِنْ نُوْرِهِ وَأَضَا ۝ وَدَخَلَ فِيْ عَقْدِ بَيْعَتِهِ

مَنْ بَقِيَ مِنَ الْخَلَائِقِ كَمَا دَخَلَ فِيْهَا مَنْ مَّضَى ۝

and the universe illuminated and glistened with his light. The rest of creation entered the bond of his loyalty,[60] just like those who did so previously.

---

[59] Some Ḥadīths have stated that he was born circumcised and without a naval (without an umbilical cord), related by Ibn Asākir, Ṭabarānī, Abū Naʿīm, Khaṭīb, some scholars are at variance regarding this.

[60] This refers to the fact that the Messenger of Allah ﷺ was sent to the whole of creation. There is a Ḥadīth narrated by Khaṭīb that when the Messenger of Allah ﷺ was born (*Sayyida*) Āmina heard a herald proclaim: 'There does not remain any creature in the world but that they have entered submissively into his authority.' This has also been cited by Abu Naʿīm on the authority of Ibn ʿAbbās, however, there is variance regarding its authenticity.

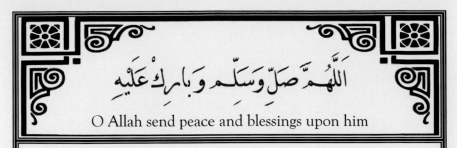

أَوَّلُ فَضِيلَةِ الْمُعْجِزَاتُ بِخُمُودِ نَارِ فَارِسَ وَسُقُوطِ الشُّرُفَاتِ ۝

وَرُمِيَتِ الشَّيَاطِينُ مِنَ السَّمَاءِ بِالشُّهُبِ الْمُحْرِقَاتِ ۝

The first excellent miracle was the extinguishing of the fire in Persia and the fall of its palaces.[61] The Shayāṭīn were pelted with shooting stars,[62]

وَرَجَعَ كُلُّ جَبَّارٍ مِنَ الْجِنِّ وَهُوَ بِصَوْلَةِ سَلْطَنَتِهِ ذَلِيلٌ خَاضِعٌ ۝

لِمَا تَأَلَّقَ مِنْ سَنَاهُ النُّورُ السَّاطِعُ ۝

and every tyrannical Jinn, while in the peak of their power became subservient and submissive. When the brilliant light beamed from his teeth,

وَأَشْرَقَ مِنْ بَهَائِهِ الضِّيَاءُ اللَّامِعُ ۝

حَتَّى عُرِضَ عَلَى الْمَرَاضِعِ ۝

and radiance blazed from his splendor,
until it was exposed to the suckling mothers.

---

61 *Shurufāt* means balconies in relation to the palaces of Chosroes, fourteen balconies collapsed. The scholars of the Prophetic *sīrah* and Ḥadīth specialists have mentioned the many amazing events that occurred at the the time of his birth, may blessings and peace be upon him such as the above, the receding of the lake of Tiberias (a city in Palestine) and the extinguishing of the fire of Persia, which had been burning constantly for a thousand years. Ibn Kathīr has cited it in his *sīrah* Vol. 1, p. 205, Ibn al-Jawzī in his '*Wafā*' vol.1, p.97 and Qasṭalānī in his '*Mawāhib*' Vol.1, p.23.

62 *Shuhubāt* can either be translated as shooting stars or meteors. Allah the Exalted states the converse of the Jinn: "*We tried, as usual, to travel to heaven in search of news but found it filled with fierce guards and meteors. We used to sit there on special seats to listen in. But anyone listening now finds a fiery meteor in wait for him.*" Qur'ān [72: 9-11]. This issue is dealt with at greater length in the *Ṣaḥīḥ* of Bukhārī.

قِيلَ: مَنْ يَكْفُلُ هَذِهِ الدُّرَّةَ الْيَتِيمَة ۝ اَلَّتِي لَا تُوجَدُ لَهَا
الْقِيمَةُ؟ قَالَتِ الطُّيُورُ: نَحْنُ نَكْفُلُهُ وَنَغْتَنِمُ هِمَّتَهُ الْعَظِيمَة

It was asked, 'Who will take care of this orphan pearl, the priceless one?' Said the birds: "We will take care of him and embrace the opportunity to perform a tremendous endeavor."

قَالَتِ الْوُحُوشُ: نَحْنُ أَوْلَى بِذَلِكَ لِكَيْ نَنَالَ شَرَفَهُ وَتَعْظِيمَة ۝
قِيلَ: يَا مَعْشَرَ الْأُمَمِ أُسْكُتُوا،

Said the beasts: "We are more entitled, so that we may honour and venerate him." It was said, "O people of the nations, be silent,

فَإِنَّ اللهَ قَدْ حَكَمَ فِي سَابِقِ حِكْمَتِهِ الْقَدِيمَة ۝ بِأَنَّ نَبِيَّهُ
مُحَمَّدًا صَلَّى اللهُ عَلَيْهِ وَسَلَّمَ يَكُونُ رَضِيعًا لِحَلِيمَةَ الْحَلِيمَة ۝

Indeed Allah has commanded with His pre-eternal Wisdom that His Prophet, Our master Muhammad will be suckled with the clemency of (Sayyida) Ḥalīma."

فَلَمَّا أَعْرَضَ عَنْهُ مَرَاضِعُ الْإِنْسِ ۝ لِمَا سَبَقَ فِي طَيِّ الْغَيْبِ

مِنَ السَّعَادَةِ لِحَلِيمَةَ بِنْتِ أَبِي ذُؤَيْب ۝

Then suckling mothers turned away from him, due to the decree in the unseen for the happiness Of (Sayyida) Ḥalīma, the daughter of Abū Dhu'aib.[63]

فَلَمَّا وَقَعَ نَظَرُهَا عَلَيْهِ ۝ بَادَرَتْ مُسْرِعَةً إِلَيْهِ ۝ وَوَضَعَتْهُ

فِي حِجْرِهَا ۝ وَضَمَّتْهُ إِلَى صَدْرِهَا ۝ فَهَشَّ لَهَا مُتَبَسِّمًا ۝

When she glanced upon him she swiftly hastened towards him, placed him in her lap and held him close in her embrace. He smiled at her kindly,

[63] She was Ḥalīma the daughter of ᶜAbdallāh ibn Ḥārith, known as Abū Zu'ayb. They were from the tribe of Banī Saᶜd and they lived over Ṭā'if. She related many accounts of the Prophet ﷺ which have been mentioned in many books of the prophetic *sīrah*. Ḥāfiẓ Ibn Ḥajar has recounted them in his *'Iṣābah'* in the first chapter. In some accounts it is mentioned that when she set her eyes upon him, she was bestowed with many favours on account of him ﷺ. She said, "Allah continually exposed many blessings that we know of, yet He still increases with His favours upon us." For futher details see *Sīrah* of Ibn Kathīr Vol.1, p.227. It has been mentioned in the narrations of Ibn Isḥāq, Ibn Rawāha, Abī Yaᶜlā, Ṭabrānī, Bayhaqī and Abū Naᶜīm that when she placed her hand upon him, he laughed with a smile, and a light emerged from him, attached to the heaven. Cited from Qasṭalānī's *'Al-Mawāhib'* p.28, though he does not mention anything regarding its authenticity.

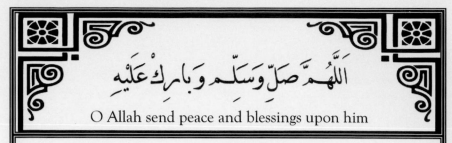

فَخَرَجَ مِنْ ثَغْرِهِ نُورٌ لَحِقَ بِالسَّمَا ۝ فَحَمَلَتْهُ إِلَى رَحْلِهَا ۝

وَارْتَحَلَتْ بِهِ إِلَى أَهْلِهَا ۝ فَلَمَّا وَصَلَتْ بِهِ إِلَى مُقَامِهَا ۝

and from his teeth emanated a light that was attached to the heaven. Then she carried him on her mount and journeyed with him to her people. And when she arrived with him at her destination,

عَايَنَتْ بَرَكَتَهُ عَلَى أَغْنَامِهَا ۝ وَكَانَتْ كُلَّ يَوْمٍ

تَرَى مِنْهُ بُرْهَانَا ۝ وَتَرْفَعُ لَهُ قَدْرًا وَشَانَا ۝

she saw his blessing upon her goats; and everyday she would witness a sign from him. She raised him with honour and esteem,

حَتَّى انْدَرَجَ فِي حُلَّةِ اللُّطْفِ وَالأَمَانِ ۝

وَدَخَلَ بَيْنَ إِخْوَتِهِ مَعَ الصِّبْيَانِ ۝

until he embodied in his vestment trustworthiness and kindness.
and joined his brothers with the boys.

اَللّٰهُمَّ صَلِّ وَسَلِّمْ وَبَارِكْ عَلَيْهِ

O Allah send peace and blessings upon him

فَبَيْنَمَا هُوَ ذَاتَ يَوْمٍ نَاءٍ عَنِ الْأَوْطَانِ ۝ إِذْ أَقْبَلَ عَلَيْهِ ثَلَاثَةُ

نَفَرٍ كَأَنَّ وُجُوهَهُمُ الشَّمْسُ وَالْقَمَرُ ۝

One day he was distant from home, when three figures approached him, whose faces were like the sun and the moon.

فَانْطَلَقَ الصِّبْيَانُ هَرَبًا ۝ وَوَقَفَ النَّبِيُّ صَلَّى اللهُ عَلَيْهِ وَسَلَّمَ

مُتَعَجِّبًا ۝ فَأَضْجَعُوهُ عَلَى الْأَرْضِ إِضْجَاعًا خَفِيفًا ۝

الْأَرْضِ إِضْجَاعًا خَفِيفًا ۝ وَشَقُّوا بَطْنَهُ شَقًّا لَطِيفًا ۝

The boys left him and fled, and the Prophet ﷺ stood in amazement. They laid him down with extreme tenderness and gently cleaved his stomach.[64]

[64] Ḥāfiẓ Ibn Kathīr said regarding the ḥadīth of cleaving the Prophetic stomach ﷺ that this ḥadīth has been related through many chains of transmissions. It belongs to the collection of famous ḥadīths and is well attested to by the scholars of *sīrah* and *maghāzī*. In the account of Muslim: 'Jibrīl cleaved his noble heart and removed from it a black clot, then he washed it in a golden vessel with the water of Zam Zam.'

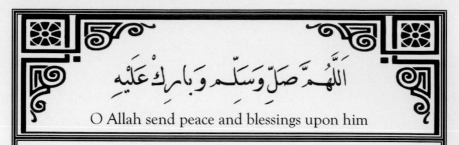

ثُمَّ أَخْرَجُوا قَلْبَ سَيِّدِ وَلَدِ عَدْنَانْ ○ وَشَرَحُوهُ

بِسِكِّينِ الْإِحْسَانِ ○ وَنَزَعُوا مِنْهُ حَظَّ الشَّيْطَانْ ○

Then, they took out the heart of the honourable son of Adnān and cut it open with the knife of excellence, and they removed from it the part of Shayṭān.[e]

وَمَلَؤُوهُ بِالْحِلْمِ وَالْعِلْمِ وَالْيَقِينِ وَالرِّضْوَانِ ○ وَأَعَادُوهُ إِلَى

مَكَانِهِ ○ قَامَ الْحَبِيبُ صَلَّى اللهُ عَلَيْهِ وَسَلَّمَ سَوِيًّا كَمَا كَانْ ○

They filled his heart with forbearance, knowledge, certainty and pleasure, then returned it to its place; then, al-Ḥabīb ﷺ stood up as healthy as before.

[e] Although this event has been mentioned in the ḥadīth, the people of Allah remind us that the Prophet was born in perfection. He was not in need of any cleansing and it is absolutely impossible for him to be susceptible to Shayṭān. The black clot has been interpreted by some scholars as being the part of mercy which would have been due to Iblīs from the Prophet since he is the mercy to all creation. Whatever the reality of the meaning is; the established creed of ahl as-Sunnah should always be brought to mind upon the pure sublimity of the Prophet as defined by Allah's testament of his inward in the verse 'And truly you are of a tremendous nature.' (68:4)

اَللّٰهُمَّ صَلِّ وَسَلِّمْ وَبَارِكْ عَلَيْهِ

O Allah send peace and blessings upon him

فَقَالَتِ الْمَلَائِكَةُ: يَا حَبِيبَ الرَّحْمَانِ لَوْ عَلِمْتَ مَا يُرَادُ بِكَ

مِنَ الْخَيْرِ ۝ لَعَرَفْتَ قَدْرَ مَنْزِلَتِكَ عَلَى الْغَيْرِ ۝

The angels said, "O Ḥabīb al-Raḥmān, had you known the blessings that are desired from you,[65] you would know the extent of your rank over others,

وَازْدَدْتَ فَرَحًا وَسُرُورًا ۝ وَبَهْجَةً وَنُورًا ۝ يَا مُحَمَّدُ

أَبْشِرْ فَقَدْ نُشِرَتْ فِي الْكَائِنَاتِ أَعْلَامُ عُلُومِكَ ۝

and would increase in happiness, joy, splendour and light. O (Sayyidinā) Muhammad, rejoice as the signs of your knowledge have spread throughout the universe,

وَتَبَاشَرَتِ الْمَخْلُوقَاتُ بِقُدُومِكَ ۝ وَلَمْ يَبْقَ شَيْءٌ مِمَّا

خَلَقَ اللّٰهُ تَعَالَى إِلَّا جَاءَ طَائِعًا ۝ وَلِمَقَالَتِكَ سَامِعًا ۝

and the creation rejoice with your arrival. Nothing remains of Allah's creation, but that it has come in compliance and in adherence to your speech.

[65] Bayhaqī narrated the Ḥadīth, wherein, the angels after the cleaving of the noble stomach, they said to him ﷺ: "O Beloved of Allah, had you known of the blessings that are desired from you, you would have been delighted." Related by Bayhaqī in his *'Dalā'il'* vol.1, p.111.

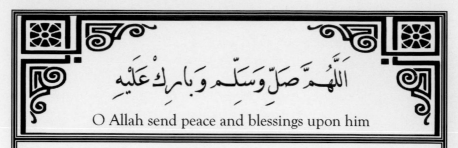

فَسَيَأْتِيكَ الْبَعِيرُ ، بِذِمَامِكَ يَسْتَجِيرُ ۝

وَالضَّبُّ وَالْغَزَالَة يَشْهَدَانِ لَكَ بِالرِّسَالَه ۝

The camel will come forth seeking refuge in your protection.
The lizard and gazelle will testify to you bearing the Message,

وَالْقَمَرُ وَالشَّجَرُ وَالذِّئْب ۝ يَنْطِقُونَ بِنُبُوَّتِكَ عَنْ قَرِيب ۝

وَمَرْكَبُكَ الْبُرَاقُ إِلَى جَمَالِكَ مُشْتَاق ۝

while the moon, the tree, and the wolf converse about your Prophethood that is near.[66] Your transport is al-Burāq, who yearns for your beauty.

---

[66] We mentioned earlier, the account of the camel seeking protection with the Prophet ﷺ. As for the gazelle and her greeting the Prophet ﷺ with her speech and testification, Ibn Kathīr holds the opinion that there is some doubt regarding this account. On the other hand al-Suyūṭī has cited the Ḥadīth with its chain of transmission in his '*Khasā'is*' vol.2, p.266, and he says, 'This Ḥadīth has many chains of transmissions that verify the authenticity of this account.' This account is not unusual for there have been occurrences of this kind, such as the tree trunk, the camel, the stones, which have been affirmed through sound transmissions, however, the grounds of possibility are unlike the grounds of proof. As for the converse of the moon and trees regarding Prophethood, it refers to their response in seeking him, and showing compliance to his command. This form of expression sets forth clearly regarding his Prophethood ﷺ and the complete support that he had, such as the splitting of the moon in two, and Allah the Exalted said: "*The Hour has drawn near and the moon has split*" Qur'ān [54:1]. All the scholars are unanimous that the splitting of the moon occurred during the time of the Prophet, may blessings and peace be upon him and his family. And we have mentioned the event of the tree and its greeting the Prophet ﷺ it acknowledged and bore witness to his Prophethood ﷺ. As for the wolf, this account is famous and has been related in many different Ḥadīths that have been cited by Aḥmad, Ibn Saᶜd, Ḥakīm and Bayhaqī. Ibn Kathīr has mentioned it in his '*Shamā'il*' p.274 and al-Suyūṭī has cited it in his '*Khasā'is*' vol.2, p.267.

وَجِبْرِيلُ شَاوُشُ مَمْلَكَتِكَ قَدْ أَعْلَنَ بِذِكْرِكَ

فِي الْآفَاقِ ۝ وَالْقَمَرُ مَأْمُورٌ لَكَ بِالْإِنْشِقَاقِ ۝

Jibrīl is the guardian of your kingdom and has pronounced your name in
the horizons. The moon is at your service by its splitting.

اَللّٰهُمَّ صَلِّ وَسَلِّمْ وَبَارِكْ عَلَيْهِ

O Allah send peace and blessings upon him

وَكُلُّ مَنْ فِي الْكَوْنِ مُتَشَوِّقٌ لِظُهُورِكَ ۝ مُنْتَظِرٌ لِإِشْرَاقِ

نُورِكَ ۝ فَبَيْنَمَا الْحَبِيبُ صَلَّى اللّٰهُ عَلَيْهِ وَسَلَّمَ مُنْصِتٌ

All those in the universe are longing for your arrival,
anticipating the rays of your light. Meanwhile al-Ḥabib ﷺ

لِسَمَاعِ تِلْكَ الْأَشْبَاحِ ۝ وَوَجْهُهُ مُتَهَلِّلٌ كَنُورِ الصِّبَاحِ ۝

إِذْ أَقْبَلَتْ حَلِيمَةُ مُعْلِنَةً بِالصِّيَاحِ تَقُولُ: وَا غَرِيبَاهُ،

is attentive to the sounds of those spirits and his face is joyful like the
radiance of the morn. Then, (Sayyida) Ḥalīma comes forth,
proclaiming aloud; "O what estrangement!"

فَقَالَتِ الْمَلَائِكَةُ: يَا مُحَمَّدُ مَا أَنْتَ بِغَرِيب ۞

بَلْ أَنْتَ مِنَ اللهِ قَرِيب ۞ وَأَنْتَ لَهُ صَفِيٌّ وَحَبِيب ۞

The angels say, "O (Sayyidinā) Muhammad you are not a stranger, rather you are by Allah most nigh, to Whom you are a beloved and an elect friend."

قَالَتْ حَلِيمَةُ: وَاوَحِيدَاه ۞ فَقَالَتِ الْمَلَائِكَةُ: يَا مُحَمَّدُ مَا

أَنْتَ بِوَحِيد ۞ بَلْ أَنْتَ صَاحِبُ التَّأْيِيد ۞

وَأَنِيسُكَ الْحَمِيدُ الْمَجِيدُ

(Sayyida) Ḥalīma says: "O his loneliness!" The angels say: "O (Sayyidinā) Muhammad you are not alone, rather you are the support and your intimate is the Most Glorious, the Most Praised;

وَإِخْوَانُكَ مِنَ الْمَلَائِكَةِ وَأَهْلِ التَّوْحِيد ۞ قَالَتْ حَلِيمَةُ:

وَايَتِيمَاهُ ۞ فَقَالَتِ الْمَلَائِكَةُ: لِلَّهِ دَرُّكَ مِنْ

يَتِيمٍ ۞ فَإِنَّ قَدْرَكَ عِنْدَ اللهِ الْعَظِيم ۞

your brothers are the angels and the people of Tawḥīd."[67] (Sayyida) Ḥalīma says: O he is an orphan!" The angels say: "To Allah belongs your orphan pearl, indeed your worth by Allah is great."

[67] The conversation is sound in essence, and its reality has been supported, but I have not found it in this context and wording.

اَللّٰهُمَّ صَلِّ وَسَلِّمْ وَبَارِكْ عَلَيْهِ

O Allah send peace and blessings upon him

فَلَمَّا رَأَتْهُ حَلِيمَةُ سَالِمًا مِنَ الْأَهْوَالِ ۞ رَجَعَتْ بِهِ مَسْرُورَةً

إِلَى الْأَطْلَالِ ۞ ثُمَّ قَصَّتْ خَبَرَهُ عَلَى بَعْضِ الْكُهَّانِ ،

When (Sayyida) Ḥalīma saw him safe from all distress, she returned with him delighted. She related his news to one of the priests,

وَأَعَادَتْ عَلَيْهِ مَا تَمَّ مِنْ أَمْرِهِ وَمَا كَانَ ۞ فَقَالَ لَهُ الْكَاهِنُ:

يَا ابْنَ زَمْزَمَ وَالْمَقَامِ ۞ وَالرُّكْنِ وَالْبَيْتِ الْحَرَامِ ۞

and told him of his affair and what had occurred.[68] The priest said to him: "O son of the Zam Zam and the Maqām, of the Ruqn and the Bait il-Ḥarām,

---

[68] The news of the priests and Rabbi's regarding the coming of the Prophet ﷺ is well known in the books of *Sīrah.* Bukhārī related on the authority of *Sayyidinā* ʿUmar ibn al-Khaṭṭāb ؓ he passed by a man and asked him of his acquaintance. He replied, "I was one of their priests in the *Jāhiliyya* period, when, there was news of his appearance ﷺ." Ibn Kathīr has mentioned much on this issue in his '*Bidāya*' with the chain of transmissions. Others have mentioned more than he has, however, they have not mentioned it in this version, and I have not come across a version as worded in this poem.

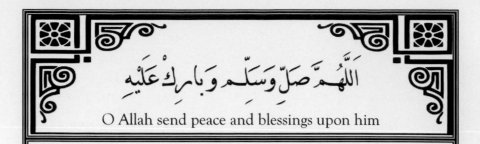

أَفِي الْيَقِظَةِ رَأَيْتَ هَذَا أَمْ فِي الْمَنَامِ ؟ فَقَالَ: بَلْ وَحُرْمَةِ

الْمَلِكِ الْعَلَّامِ شَاهَدْتُهُمْ كِفَاحًا لَا أَشُكُّ فِي ذَلِكَ وَلَا أُضَامُ ۝

was it in a wakeful state that you saw this, or in a dream?" He said: "Indeed by the Sanctity of the All Knowing King, I witnessed them while striving, I do not doubt this nor am I unjust."

فَقَالَ لَهُ الْكَاهِنُ: أَبْشِرْ أَيُّهَا الْغُلَامُ ۝ فَأَنْتَ صَاحِبُ

الْأَعْلَامِ ۝ وَنُبُوَّتُكَ لِلْأَنْبِيَاءِ قُفْلٌ وَخِتَامٌ ۝

The priest said, "Rejoice O Young One, for you possess the signs; your Prophethood is a lock and a seal for the Prophets.

عَلَيْكَ يَنْزِلُ جِبْرِيلُ ۝ وَعَلَى بِسَاطِ الْقُدْسِ يُخَاطِبُكَ

الْجَلِيلُ ۝ وَمَنْ ذَا الَّذِي يَحْصُرُ مَا حَوَيْتَ مِنَ التَّفْضِيلِ ۝

To you descends Jibrīl, and upon the Divine carpet the Majesty addresses you, the One who encompasses the virtues that you possess.

وَعَنْ بَعْضِ وَصْفِ مَعْنَاكَ يَقْصُرُ لِسَانُ الْمَادِحِ الْمُطِيلِ ۝

To describe your significance, the tongue of the eloquent eulogist falls short.

اللّٰهُمَّ صَلِّ وَسَلِّمْ وَبَارِكْ عَلَيْهِ

O Allah send peace and blessings upon him

وَكَانَ صَلَّى اللهُ عَلَيْهِ وَسَلَّمَ أَحْسَنَ النَّاسِ خَلْقًا وَخُلُقًا ۝

وَأَهْدَاهُمْ إِلَى الْحَقِّ طُرُقًا ، وَكَانَ خُلُقُهُ الْقُرْآن ۝

The Messenger of Allah ﷺ, was the best of people, by form and by nature.[69] He guided them to the path of Truth.[70]
His character was the Qur'ān[71]

وَشِيمَتُهُ الْغُفْرَان ۝ يَنْصَحُ لِلْإِنْسَان ۝ وَيَفْسَحُ فِي

الْإِحْسَان ۝ وَيَعْفُو عَنِ الذَّنْبِ إِذَا كَانَ فِي حَقِّهِ وَسَبَبِه ۝

and he was accustomed to forgiveness.[72] He would counsel the people, and was liberal in his favours.
He would forgive faults when he was wronged,

---

[69] Related in Bukhārī on the authority of Barā' ibn ᶜĀzib, who said, "He ﷺ was the best of people by form and nature." And also on the same authority, he said, "The Messenger of Allah ﷺ was the best of people in beauty and the best of them in character." Narrated in Muslim and Bukhārī.

[70] Meaning that he informed them of the truth, to which the sound Ḥadīth alludes: "I am the most knowledgeable, most conscious and most fearful of Allah amongst you."

[71] (*Sayyida*) ᶜĀ'isha ﷺ said: "His character was the Qur'ān, his contentment was the contentment of the Qur'ān, and his displeasure was the displeasure of the Qur'ān." A sound Ḥadīth.

[72] He would pardon, forgive and was very generous with gifts; these are very significant traits and qualities that have been affirmed in the sound Ḥadīth to which there is no doubt as the Exalted says: "*Indeed you have a great character.*" [Qur'ān 68:4] This has been exposed in the Prophetic Sunna, when (*Sayyida*) ᶜĀ'isha said:

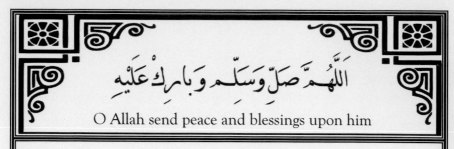

وَإِذَا أُضِيعَ حَقُّ اللهِ لَمْ يَقُمْ أَحَدٌ لِغَضَبِهِ ○

مَنْ رَآهُ بَدِيهَةً هَابَهُ ○ وَإِذَا دَعَاهُ الْمِسْكِينُ أَجَابَهُ ○

but if the right of Allah were transgressed, no one would be able to withstand his anger. Whoever saw him was filled with awe.[73] When a needy called to him, he would respond.[74]

"The Prophet ﷺ did not choose a matter only that he chose the easier of the two that did not have a sin involved. If there was a sin therein, he was the most distant of people from it. And he ﷺ did not take revenge for his own sake, but if the sanctity of Allah had been transgressed, he would take revenge for the sake of Allah." And his saying e, "O Allah, guide my people for they know not." And when they distressed him on the Day of Uḥud, for which they did not even fear, he said, "Go for you are free."

[73] Anyone who saw him was filled with awe, out of delight on seeing him ﷺ. (*Sayyidinā*) ᶜAlī ؓ said, "One who saw him was filled with reverence" related by Tirmīdhī in his '*Shamā'il*' Others have said that 'People sat with reverence in his gathering', related by Abū Dāwud in '*Nasīm al-Riyāḍ*' vol. 2, p. 117. Amr ibn al-Ās said regarding the presence of the Messenger of Allah ﷺ "I was unable to set my eyes upon him out of reverence for him. Were you to ask me to describe him, I would be unable as I could not set my eyes upon him." Related by Muslim in his *Saḥīḥ'*. Ibn Abī Ḥāla said, "When he spoke, his gathering was so still as though there were birds upon their heads." Related by Tirmīdhī, Ibn Saᶜd and Tabrānī.

[74] On the authority of Anas ؓ who said: "The Messenger of Allah ﷺ would respond to the call of a person." Related by Abū Dāwud and Bayhaqī, and a similar version by Tirmīdhī and Ibn Mājah.

يَقُولُ الحَقَّ وَلَوْ كَانَ مُرًّا ۝ وَلَا يُضْمِرُ مُسْلِمٍ غِشًّا وَلَا ضُرًّا ۝

مَنْ نَظَرَ فِي وَجْهِهِ عَلِمَ أَنَّهُ لَيْسَ بِوَجْهِ كَذَّاب ۝

He would speak the truth even if it were bitter.[75] Never would he deceive a Muslim, or harm them.[76] Whoever looked upon his blessed face knew that it was not the face of a liar.[77]

وَكَانَ صَلَّى اللهُ عَلَيْهِ وَسَلَّمَ لَيْسَ بِغَمَّازٍ وَلَا عَيَّاب ۝ إِذَا سُرَّ

فَكَأَنَّ وَجْهَهُ قِطْعَةُ قَمَر ۝ وَإِذَا كَلَّمَ النَّاسَ فَكَأَنَّمَا يَجْنُونَ

مِنْ كَلَامِهِ أَحْلَى ثَمَر ۝

The Blessed Prophet ﷺ was not a faultfinder.[78] When he was joyful, it was as though his blessed face was a phase of the moon.[79] When he spoke to the people,[80] they would reap the sweetest fruit from his speech.

---

[75] This statement does not require any proof, as the situations in his battles are more evident than the sun at midday. Hence, if one were to violate the laws of Allah he would become very angry, as mentioned in the Ḥadīth of Abī Ḥāla, "The Messenger of Allah ﷺ did not refrain from truth, neither did he disregard it when concerning others." Related by Tirmīdhī.

[76] This statement does not require proof either, how would he deceive when he himself would say, "One who deceives us is not from us." And "The Muslim is the one with whose hands and tongue the Muslims are safe." It has also been mentioned that he would not censure anyone, humiliate or seek out his or her faults. Related by Ḥassan Ibn ᶜAlī on the authority of Hind Abī Ḥāla, it is cited in the *Shamā'il* of Tirmīdhī, the *Sunan* of Bayhaqī and by Tabarānī.

[77] ᶜAbdallāh ibn Salām said: "I went to the Prophet ﷺ and when I looked into his face I knew that it was not the face of a liar" Related by Tirmīdhī and he said it is sound.

[78] Ibn Abī Ḥāla said in his description: "The Messenger of Allah ﷺ was not harsh, rude, unreasonable, a faultfinder, or excessive in praise." Related by Tirmīdhī in his *Shamā'il* vol.1, p.166. It has also been related by Ibn Saᶜd Bayhaqī, Tabrānī, Qādī ᶜIyād in his '*Al-Shifā*".

وَإِذَا تَبَسَّمَ تَبَسَّمَ عَنْ مِثْلِ حَبِّ الْغَمَامِ ۝

وَإِذَا تَكَلَّمَ فَكَأَنَّمَا الدُّرَّ يَسْقُطُ مِنْ ذَلِكَ الْكَلَامِ ۝

When he smiled, his smile was like the whiteness of hailstones.[81]
When he spoke, it was like pearls emanating from that speech.

---

[79] On the authority of Kaᶜb ibn Mālik who said, "When the Messenger of Allah ﷺ smiled, his face would illuminate as though it was a phase of the moon" Narrated in Bukhārī.

[80] His speech ﷺ would enter the hearts of the people, they loved to hear him, and they were delighted by it. His speech has been described that it was concise, each word could be separated, he was neither excessive nor too brief. He would remain silent, and only speak when the need arose, he would open and end his speech with the *Basmallah*. Ibn Abī Ḥāla said in a very famous and lengthy Ḥadīth on the authority of Ibn ᶜAbbās that when he ﷺ spoke light could be seen emanating from between his teeth. Related by Tirmīdhī, Dāramī, Tabrānī. (*Sayyida*) ᶜĀ'isha ﷺ said that, "His speech was distinct, one who heard it could understand it." Related by Abū Dāwud. Anas ﷺ with him, said: "He would repeat the speech three times, in order to be understood" Narrated in Tirmīdhī. Jābir ﷺ said: "There was *tartīl* (to articulate slowly, carefully and precisely) in the speech of the Messenger of Allah ﷺ." Narrated by Abū Dāwud. On the authority of Abū Qarsafah, who said: "When we pledged allegiance with the Messenger of Allah ﷺ my mother and aunt said to me, 'O Dear son, we have not seen a man more beautiful by face, or neater in clothing or softer in speech than him, it's as though light emerges from his mouth." Related by Tabarānī.

[81] On the authority of Jābir ibn Samra who said, "The Messenger of Allah ﷺ did not laugh only that it was a smile." Cited by Tirmīdhī. This was usually the way he laughed, however, there are some accounts that describe the exposure of his teeth when he laughed, I'm sure there is no exaggeration in this, although, in my opinion, I believe that he laughed and his teeth could almost be seen. It has been mentioned in *'Al-Shifā"* on the authority of Bayhaqī, "When his teeth were exposed on smiling it was like a flash of lightening and like hailstones."

وَإِذَا تَحَدَّثَ فَكَأَنَّ الْمِسْكَ يَخْرُجُ مِنْ فِيهِ ۝

وَإِذَا مَرَّ بِطَرِيقٍ عُرِفَ مِنْ طِيبِهِ أَنَّهُ قَدْ مَرَّ فِيهِ ۝

When he conversed, it was as if the fragrance of musk emitted from his mouth. When he passed by a street, it was known from his fragrance that he had passed by.

وَإِذَا جَلَسَ فِي مَجْلِسٍ بَقِي طِيبُهُ فِيهِ أَيَّامًا وَإِنْ تَغَيَّبْ ۝

وَيُوجَدُ مِنْهُ أَحْسَنُ طِيبٍ وَإِنْ لَمْ يَكُنْ قَدْ تَطَيَّبْ ۝

When he sat in a gathering, his blessed fragrance remained for a day, even after he had left. There was no fragrance better than his fragrance, even if he had not perfumed himself.[82]

وَإِذَا مَشَى بَيْنَ أَصْحَابِهِ فَكَأَنَّهُ الْقَمَرُ بَيْنَ النُّجُومِ الزُّهْرِ ۝

وَإِذَا أَقْبَلَ لَيْلًا فَكَأَنَّ النَّاسَ مِنْ نُورِهِ فِي أَوَانِ الظُّهْرِ ۝

His walking amongst his Companions was like the moon amongst the shining stars. Upon nightfall, with his light, it was as though people were in broad daylight.[83]

[82] Anas ؓ said: "I never smelt a fragrance more fragrant than the perspiration of the Messenger of Allah ﷺ" narrated by Bukhārī and Muslim. Jābir ؓ said, "No one would pass through a street, wherein the Messenger of Allah ﷺ had walked only that he would know this by the fragrance of his perspiration." Narrated by Dāramī and Bukhārī in '*Tārīkh ul-Kabīr*' He also said that when the Messenger of Allah ﷺ touched his cheek (the cheek of Jābir) he said, "I found his hand cool and fragrant as if he had just removed it from a bottle of perfume." Narrated by Muslim. Others have said, "Had he applied perfume or not, when he shook someone's hand, it's fragrance would remain for a whole day, and when he placed his hand on the head of a child his fragrance would be distinguished amongst the other children." Related by Bayhaqī and Abū Naᶜīm.

وَكَانَ صَلَّى اللهُ عَلَيْهِ وَسَلَّمَ أَجْوَدَ بِالْخَيْرِ مِنَ الرِّيحِ الْمُرْسَلَه ۝

وَكَانَ يَرْفُقُ بِالْيَتِيمِ وَالْأَرْمَلَه ۝

The Messenger of Allah ﷺ was more generous than the swiftness of wind;[84] He would befriend the orphan and the widow.[85]

يَقُولُ بَعْضُ وَاصِفِيهِ: مَا رَأَيْتُ مِنْ ذِي لِمَّةٍ سَوْدَاءَ فِي حُلَّةٍ

حَمْرَاءَ أَحْسَنَ مِنْ رَسُولِ اللهِ صَلَّى اللهُ عَلَيْهِ وَسَلَّمَ ۝

Some of those that described him said, "I have not seen one with[86] black hair on a red robe more beautiful than the Messenger of Allah ﷺ."

---

[83] Abī Khathāma said, "The Messenger of Allah ﷺ had the most radiant forehead. When it was visible through his hair or in the night or when his face was seen amongst the people, his forehead would appear as though it was a resplendent glowing light." And they would say that he is the Messenger of Allah ﷺ."

[84] The swiftness of his generosity means that he was swifter than the wind in doing good, like how the wind is not prevented by anything while it is blowing. This Ḥadīth has been mentioned in Bukhārī and Muslim, there is also the version that says, "He was the most generous person and he would give gifts like one who does not fear poverty." And, "He was the more generous in good works than the blowing wind," as mentioned in Bukhārī. (*Sayyidinā*) ᶜAlī ؓ said, "The Messenger of Allah ﷺ was the most generous of heart, the most truthful in speech, the most softest in disposition and the most generous in companionship. One who saw him was struck with awe, one who associated with him thought that he loved them the most, of those that praise him would say I have not seen anyone like him, not before him nor after him." Related by Tirmīdhī.

[85] He ﷺ would instruct people to be charitable with orphans and widows, by saying, "I and the supporter of an orphan are like these two in heaven" [indicating with the index and the middle fingers]. Related by Muslim. And he urged making effort for the widow, by saying, "The one who strives for the widow and the poor are like those who fight in the way of Allah." Related by Bukhārī and Muslim.

[86] Al-Barā' ؓ said, "I saw him in a red robe, and I have never seen anyone more beautiful than him." Related by Muslim.

اَللَّهُمَّ صَلِّ وَسَلِّمْ وَبَارِكْ عَلَيْهِ

O Allah send peace and blessings upon him

وَقِيلَ لِبَعْضِهِمْ: كَأَنَّ وَجْهَهُ الْقَمَرُ، فَقَالَ: بَلْ

أَضْوَأُ مِنَ الْقَمَرِ إِذَا لَمْ يَحُلْ دُونَهُ الْغَمَامُ قَدْ غَشِيَهُ الْجَلَالُ ۝

It was said to one of them: "His face is like the moon."[87] He was responded: "Rather his face is more luminous than the moon, since the clouds are not permitted to cover his majesty."

---

[87] Many accounts have been related by the Companions who described the Messenger of Allah ﷺ with a radiant face, resplendent and bashful, shining with brilliance, and emanating light and a manifest splendour. There were some Companions who drew parallels of his light ﷺ with the sun, and others likened it to the moon, others likened the brilliance of his face to the radiance of the moon. As in the Ḥadīth of Ḥassan ibn ᶜAlī, who said ﷺ, "The Messenger of Allah ﷺ was majestic, esteemed, and his face, may blessings and peace be upon him radiated like the full moon." Related by Tirmīdhī. Jābir ibn Samra looked at him on the night of a full moon, he said, "I began to look at him and at the moon, and to me he looked more beautiful than the moon." Related by Tirmīdhī. A man asked Barā' Ibn ᶜĀzib, "Was the face of the Messenger of Allah ﷺ him like a sword?" He replied, "No rather it was like the moon." Related by Bukhārī and Tirmīdhī. Jābir said, "It was round like the sun and the moon." Related by Muslim. Sayyida ᶜĀ'isha ﷺ said, "The Messenger of Allah ﷺ was the most beautiful, and the most radiant in complexion. No one described him but that they likened his face to the full moon, the drops of sweat on his face were like pearls, and more fragrant than the most fragrant musk." Related by Abū Naᶜīm. Rabi' bint Maᶜūdh was asked to describe the Messenger of Allah ﷺ. She said, "O My dear son, had you seen him you would have seen the rising sun." Related by Tirmīdhī and Bayhaqī. Abū Huraira said, "As if the sun was passing over his face." Related by Tirmīdhii. Umm Maᶜbad said, "I saw a man with brilliance, beautiful disposition, a handsome face and graceful." Related by Bayhaqī, Hākim.

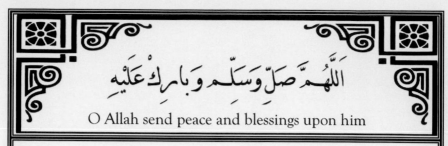

وَانْتَهَى إِلَيْهِ الْكَمَالُ ۝ قَالَ بَعْضُ وَاصِفِيهِ:

مَا رَأَيْتُ قَبْلَهُ وَلَا بَعْدَهُ مِثْلَهُ ۝

He was the optimum of perfection; and he was described by one of them,
who said, "I have not seen anyone like him,
neither before nor after him."[88]

فَيَعْجِزُ لِسَانُ الْبَلِيغِ إِذَا أَرَادَ أَنْ يُحْصِي فَضْلَهُ ۝ فَسُبْحَانَ مَنْ

خَصَّهُ صَلَّى اللهُ عَلَيْهِ وَسَلَّمَ بِالْمَحَلِّ الْأَسْنَى ۝

وَأَسْرَى بِهِ إِلَى قَابَ قَوْسَيْنِ أَوْ أَدْنَى ۝

The tongue of the eloquent falls short when he wants to enumerate his
virtues. So glory be to the One Who distinguished him with the most
sublime rank and made him travel by night to two bow's length or nearer.

وَأَيَّدَهُ بِالْمُعْجِزَاتِ الَّتِي لَا تُحْصَى ۝

وَوَافَاهُ مِنْ خِصَالِ الْكَمَالِ بِمَا يَجِلُّ أَنْ يُسْتَقْصَى ۝

He affirmed him with countless miracles and honoured him
with characteristics that surpass investigation.

---

[88] Sayyidinā ʿAlī ؓ said, "I did not see anyone like him, not before him nor after
him." Related by Aḥmad.

وَأَعْطَاهُ خَمْسًا لَمْ يُعْطِهِنَّ أَحَدًا قَبْلَهُ ۝ وَآتَاهُ جَوَامِعَ الْكَلِمِ

فَلَمْ يُدْرِكْ أَحَدٌ فَضْلَه ۝ وَكَانَ لَهُ صَلَّى اللهُ عَلَيْهِ وَسَلَّمَ

He was bestowed with five attributes that had not been granted to anyone before him.[89] He was given concise speech,[90] no one knew of its excellence. He ﷺ,

فِي كُلِّ مَقَامٍ مَقَال ۝ وَلِكُلِّ كَمَالٍ مِنْهُ كَمَال ۝ لَا يَحُولُ

فِي سُؤَالٍ وَلَا جَوَاب ۝ وَلَا يَجُولُ لِسَانُهُ إِلَّا فِي صَوَاب ۝

had appropriate speech for every context;[91] every perfect [attribute] of his was complete. No one debated [with him] in a question or an answer; his tongue was only engaged with rightness.

---

[89] This is evident through him ﷺ who said, "I was given five [attributes] that no one bestowed with before me. I was given victory by having fear cast [into the enemies hearts] by a distance of a month. The earth has been purified for me and made as a mosque so that wherever one wishes they may pray. Booty has been made lawful for me, which was not lawful for any of [the prophets] before me. And I have been given the Intercession. Every Prophet was sent to his people and the Messenger of Allah, ﷺ was sent to all of mankind." Narrated in Bukhārī and Muslim.

[90] His concise speech (*jawāmiʿ il kalimi*), this is when a sentence is vast in meaning with many benefits, but is expressed in a few words. The Messenger of Allah ﷺ said, "I was sent with concise speech." Related in Bukhārī and Muslim.

[91] Ibn Abī Ḥāla mentioned in a famous Ḥadīth, "The Messenger of Allah ﷺ did not speak unnecessarily."

اَللّٰهُمَّ صَلِّ وَسَلِّمْ وَبَارِكْ عَلَيْهِ

O Allah send peace and blessings upon him

وَمَا عَسَى أَنْ يُقَالَ فِيمَنْ وَصَفَهُ الْقُرْآنُ ۝ وَأَعْرَبَ

عَنْ فَضَائِلِهِ التَّوْرَاةُ وَالْإِنْجِيلُ وَالزَّبُورُ وَالْفُرْقَانُ ۝

It only seemed possible to describe him as the Qur'ān.[92] His virtues were stated in the Torah, the Bible, the Psalms and the Qur'ān.[93]

وَجَمَعَ اللهُ لَهُ بَيْنَ رُؤْيَتِهِ وَكَلَامِهِ ۝

وَقَرَنَ اسْمَهُ مَعَ اسْمِهِ تَنْبِيهًا عَلَى عُلُوِّ مَقَامِهِ ۝

For him, Allah brought together His vision and His speech.[94] He linked his name with His,[95] as a sign to the greatness of his prestige.

---

[92] As the Qur'ān described him, like Allah's saying: "*Indeed you have an exalted character.*"

[93] There is no doubt that the Torah and the Bible had stated many virtues of the Prophet ﷺ and of his nation, and the Book that would be revealed to him. There was also mention of the period of his Prophethood, and Allah the Exalted said, "*Those who follow the Messenger, the unlettered Prophet, who they find written about in their Torah and Bible.*" And *"That is their example in the Torah and their example in the Bible..."*

[94] This is in reference to the night of the Ascension, indeed, he heard and he saw, whereby we have no knowledge of its modality and there was no limitation that night; this is the opinion of the *Ahl al-Sunna wa'l Jamāᶜa.*

[95] Mujāhid said with regards to the verse "*We raised your mention*" that it is Allah's saying 'I will not be mentioned only that you will be mentioned with Me." Ibn Kathīr has mentioned this on the authority of Ibn Jarīr, Abū Yaᶜlā, Ibn Abī Hātim.

وَجَعَلَهُ رَحْمَةً لِلْعَالَمِينَ وَنُورًا ۝

وَمَلأَ بِمَوْلِدِهِ الْقُلُوبَ سُرُورًا ۝

He made him a Mercy and a Light for all the universes,[96]
and filled the hearts with delight with his blessed birth.

The verses of Hassan's poetry support this: *'God joined the name of His Prophet with His, thus the Muezzin proclaims in the five; 'I testify…' He was advanced by his name to exaltation, on the Throne (ʿArsh) he is the praised (Maḥmūd) and this is Muhammad.'*

[96] The Exalted said: "*I have only sent him as a mercy to mankind*" And *Sayyidinā* ʿAbbās ﷺ composed in verse: 'When you were born the earth radiated, and with your light the horizons illuminated. And we are in that light in the brightness, and the paths of guidance are glowing.'

يَا بَدْرَ تِمٍّ حَازَ كُلَّ كَمَالِ

مَاذَا يُعَبِّرُ عَنْ عُلَاكَ مَقَالِي

O full moon, that bears complete perfection,
what can my speech express of your sublimity.

أَنْتَ الَّذِي أَشْرَقْتَ فِي أُفُقِ الْعُلَى

فَمَحَوْتَ بِالْأَنْوَارِ كُلَّ ضَلَالِ

You are the one who shone in the high horizons;
and erased with your lights every deviation.

وَبِكَ اسْتَنَارَ الْكَوْنُ يَا عَلَمَ الْهُدَى

بِالنُّورِ وَالْإِنْعَامِ وَالْإِفْضَالِ

By you, the universe radiates, O Token of guidance,
with light, favours and excellence.

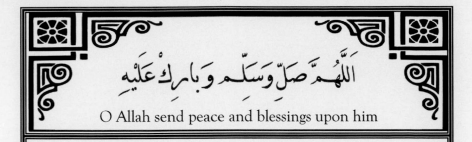

صَلَّى عَلَيْكَ اللهُ رَبِّي دَائِمًا

أَبَدًا مَعَ الإِبْكَارِ وَالآصَالِ

May Allah, my Lord send peace upon you always and forever,
in the mornings and the evenings,

وَعَلَى جَمِيعِ الآلِ وَالأَصْحَابِ مَنْ

قَدْ خَصَّهُمْ رَبُّ الْعُلَى بِكَمَالِ

with all the family and the Companions,
whom the Exalted Lord has chosen for perfection.

اَللّٰهُمَّ صَلِّ وَسَلِّمْ وَبَارِكْ عَلَيْهِ

O Allah send peace and blessings upon him

بِسْمِ اللهِ الرَّحْمٰنِ الرَّحِيمِ

اَلْحَمْدُ لِلّٰهِ رَبِّ الْعَالَمِينَ (اَللّٰهُمَّ) صَلِّ وَسَلِّمْ عَلَى

سَيِّدِنَا مُحَمَّدٍ وَعَلَى آلِهِ وَصَحْبِهِ أَجْمَعِينَ ،

All praise belongs to Allah, the Lord of the worlds. O Allah send peace and blessings upon Sayyidinā Muhammad, his family and all of his Companions.

جَعَلَنِي اللهُ وَإِيَّاكُمْ مِمَّنْ يَسْتَوْجِبُ شَفَاعَتَهُ وَيَرْجُو

بِذَلِكَ رَحْمَتَهُ وَرَأْفَتَهُ ، (اَللّٰهُمَّ) بِحُرْمَةِ هَذَا النَّبِيِّ الْكَرِيمِ ،

May Allah make you and I of those upon whom his intercession is binding, and the mercy and compassion of Allah is hoped for. O Allah, by the honour of this noble Prophet,

وَآلِهِ الطَّاهِرِينَ ، وَأَصْحَابِهِ السَّالِكِينَ ، عَلَى نَهْجِهِ الْقَوِيمِ ،

اِجْعَلْنَا مِنْ خِيَارِ أُمَّتِهِ ، وَاسْتُرْنَا بِذَيْلِ حُرْمَتِهِ ،

his family and his Companions, who travelled upon his straight path. Make us from the elect of his ummah, and cover us under the garment of his sanctity.

وَاحْشُرْنَا غَدًا فِي زُمْرَتِهِ ، وَاسْتَعْمِلْ أَلْسِنَتَنَا فِي مَدْحِهِ وَ

نُصْرَتِهِ ، وَأَحْيِنَا مُتَمَسِّكِيْنَ بِسُنَّتِهِ وَطَاعَتِهِ ،

وَأَمِتْنَا عَلَى حُبِّهِ وَجَمَاعَتِهِ ،

Gather us tomorrow, in his group and use our tongues to praise and support him. Make us live, adherent to his Sunnah and in compliance to him. And make us die, O Allah, with his love and congregation.

(اَللّٰهُمَّ) أَدْخِلْنَا مَعَهُ الْجَنَّةَ فَإِنَّهُ أَوَّلُ مَنْ يَدْخُلُهَا ،

وَأَنْزِلْنَا مَعَهُ فِي قُصُوْرِهَا فَإِنَّهُ أَوَّلُ مَنْ يَنْزِلُهَا ،

O Allah, enter us into heaven with him; indeed, he is the first of those who will enter. And reside us with him in its palaces, indeed, he will be the first of those to reside.

وَارْحَمْنَا يَوْمَ يَشْفَعُ لِلْخَلَائِقِ فَتَرْحَمُهَا ، (اَللّٰهُمَّ) ارْزُقْنَا

زِيَارَتَهُ فِي كُلِّ حِيْنٍ ، وَلَا تَجْعَلْنَا مِنَ الْغَافِلِيْنَ عَنْكَ وَلَا عَنْهُ

قَدْرَ سِنَه ،

Have mercy upon us, on the day when there will be intercession for the creation, and have mercy upon them. O Allah, endow us with his visit at all times, and do not make us of those that are heedless of You, or of him for one moment.

(اَللّٰهُمَّ) لاَ تَجْعَلْ فِي مَجْلِسِنَا هٰذَا أَحَدًا إِلاَّ غَسَلْتَ بِمَاءِ التَّوْبَةِ ذُنُوْبَه، وَسَتَرْتَ بِرِدَاءِ الْمَغْفِرَةِ عُيُوْبَه،

O Allah, make there not be anyone in this gathering of ours, but that he is washed with the water of repentance of sins, and covered with the cloak of forgiveness of faults.

(اَللّٰهُمَّ) إِنَّهُ كَانَ مَعَنَا فِي السَّنَةِ الْمَاضِيةِ إِخْوَانٌ مَنَعَهُمُ الْقَضَاءُ مِنَ الْوُصُوْلِ إِلَى مِثْلِهَا، فَلاَ تَحْرِمْهُمْ ثَوَابَ هٰذِهِ اللَّيْلَةِ وَفَضْلَهَا،

O Allah, those brothers that were with us last year, who have been prevented by Your decree to attend, may they receive the same. Do not deprive them of the reward and excellence of this moment.

(اَللّٰهُمَّ) ارْحَمْنَا إِذَا صِرْنَا مِنْ أَصْحَابِ الْقُبُوْرِ، وَوَفِّقْنَا لِعَمَلٍ صَالِحٍ يَبْقَى سَنَاهُ عَلَى مَمَرِّ الدُّهُوْرِ،

O Allah, have mercy upon us, when we become the people of the grave. Grant us success in performing righteous deeds, and may its brilliance remain with us through the passage of time.

(اَللّٰهُمَّ) اجْعَلْنَا لآلاَئِكَ ذَاكِرِيْنَ، وَلِنَعْمَائِكَ شَاكِرِيْنَ، وَلِيَوْمِ لِقَائِكَ مِنَ الذَّاكِرِيْنَ، وَأَحْيِنَا بِطَاعَتِكَ مَشْغُوْلِيْنَ،

O Allah, make us of those that remember Your favours, of those that are grateful for Your blessings, and of those who remember the Day of meeting with You. Make us live, occupied in Your obedience.

وَإِذَا تَوَفَّيْتَنَا فَتَوَفَّنَا غَيْرَ مَفْتُونِينَ ، وَلَا مَخْذُولِينَ ،

وَاخْتِمْ لَنَا مِنْكَ بِخَيْرٍ أَجْمَعِينَ ، (اَللّٰهُمَّ) اكْفِنَا شَرَّ الظَّالِمِينَ ،

When we die, make us die without tribulation or disappointment, and make our ending by You, with all good. O Allah, suffice us for the evil of the wrongdoers,

وَاجْعَلْنَا مِنْ فِتْنَةِ هٰذِهِ الدُّنْيَا سَالِمِينَ ، (اَللّٰهُمَّ) اجْعَلْ هٰذَا

الرَّسُولَ الْكَرِيمَ لَنَا شَفِيعًا ، وَارْزُقْنَا يَوْمَ الْقِيَامَةِ مَقَامًا رَفِيعًا

and keep us safe from the trials of the world. O Allah, make this honourable Messenger an intercessor for us, and by him bestow us with an exalted rank on the Day of Judgment.

(اَللّٰهُمَّ) اسْقِنَا مِنْ حَوْضِ نَبِيِّكَ مُحَمَّدٍ صَلَّى اللّٰهُ عَلَيْهِ وَسَلَّمَ

شَرْبَةً هَنِيئَةً لَا نَظْمَأُ بَعْدَهَا أَبَدًا ، وَاحْشُرْنَا تَحْتَ لِوَائِهِ غَدًا

O Allah, give us to drink, a pleasurable drink from the Hawd of Your Prophet ﷺ after which, we will never thirst. And gather us under his banner, tomorrow.

(اَللّٰهُمَّ) اغْفِرْ لَنَا بِهِ ، وَلِآبَائِنَا وَلِأُمَّهَاتِنَا ، وَمَشَائِخِنَا وَ

لِمُعَلِّمِينَا ، وَذَوِي الْحُقُوقِ عَلَيْنَا ، وَلِمَنْ أَجْرَى هٰذِهِ الْخَيْرَ

By his worth, forgive us, our parents, our elders, our teachers, those who have rights over us and the one who carried out this good,

فِي هَذِهِ السَّاعَةِ ، وَلِجَمِيعِ الْمُؤمِنِينَ وَالْمُؤْمِنَاتِ ، وَالْمُسْلِمِينَ

وَالْمُسْلِمَاتِ ، الْأَحْيَاءِ مِنْهُمْ وَالأَمْوَات ،

at this moment, and all the believing men and women, the Muslim men and women, the living from them and the deceased. For You are the

مُجِيبَ الدَّعَوَاتِ وَقَاضِي الحَاجَاتِ ، إِنَّكَ

وَغَافِرُ الذُّنُوبِ وَالْخَطِيئَاتِ ، يَا أَرْحَمَ الرَّاحِمِينَ ،

Answerer of prayer the Fulfiller of needs. You are the Forgiver of sins and errors. O The Most Merciful.

وَصَلَّى اللهُ عَلَى سَيِّدِنَا مُحَمَّدٍ وَعَلَى آلِهِ وَصَحْبِهِ وَسَلَّمَ

وَالْحَمْدُ لِلَّهِ رَبِّ الْعَالَمِينَ ،

May the peace and blessings of Allah be upon our master Muhammad, his family, and his Companions. All Praise belongs to Allah, the Lord of the worlds.

سُبْحَانَ رَبِّكَ رَبِّ الْعِزَّةِ عَمَّا يَصِفُونَ

وَسَلَامٌ عَلَى الْمُرْسَلِينَ وَالْحَمْدُ لِلَّهِ رَبِّ الْعَالَمِينَ ۝

Glory be to your Lord, the Lord of Might, beyond anything they describe. Peace be upon the messengers. All Praise belongs to Allah the Lord of the worlds.

Salutations before the Mawlid

يا رَبِّ صَلِّ عَلٰى مُحَمَّد

يا رَبِّ صَلِّ عَلَيْهِ وَسَلِّمْ

O Lord send blessings upon (Sayyidina) Muhammad
O Lord send blessings and peace upon him

يا رَبِّ بَلِّغْهُ الْوَسِيْلَة

يا رَبِّ خُصَّهُ بِالْفَضِيْلَهْ

O Lord make him the intermediary
O Lord bestow upon him with great honour

يا رَبِّ وَارْضَ عَنِ الصَّحَابَه

يا رَبِّ وَارْضَ عَنِ السُّلَالَهْ

O Lord be pleased with the Companions
O Lord be pleased with his descendents

يا رَبِّ وَارْضَ عَنِ الْمَشَائِخْ

يا رَبِّ فَارْحَمْ وَالِدِيْنَا

O Lord be pleased with the mashaikh
O Lord have mercy upon our parents

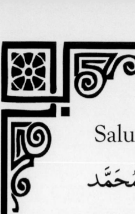

يا رَبِّ وَارْحَمْنا جَمِيْعًا

يا رَبِّ وَارْحَمْ كُلَّ مُسْلِمْ

O Lord have mercy upon us all
O Lord have mercy upon every Muslim

يا رَبِّ وَاغْفِرْ لِكُلِّ مُذْنِبٍ

يا رَبِّ لَاتَقْطَعْ رَجَانَا

O Lord forgive every sinful one
O Lord do not sever our hopes

يا رَبِّ يَاسَامِعْ دُعَانَا

يا رَبِّ بَلِّغْنَا نَزُوْرُهْ

O Lord, O the One Who hears our supplications
O Lord grant us so that we can visit him

يا رَبِّ تَغْشَانَا بِنُوْرِهِ

يا رَبِّ حِفْظَانَكْ وَاَمَانَكْ

O Lord envelope us with his light
O Lord protect us and keep us secure

يا رَبِّ وَاسْكِنَّا جِـنَانَكْ

يا رَبِّ اَجِرْنَا مِ عَذَابِكْ

O Lord give us to drink from Your gardens
O Lord protect us from Your punishment

يا رَبِّ وَارْزُقْنَا اَلشَّهَادَةْ

يا رَبِّ حِـطْنَا بِالسَّـــعَادَةْ

O Lord grant us the testification
O Lord grant us felicity

يا رَبِّ وَاصْلِحْ كُلَّ مُصْلِحٍ

يا رَبِّ وَاكْفِ كُلَّ مُؤْذِيْ

O Lord correct us with every good
O Lord suffice us for every one that causes harm

يا رَبِّ نَخْـتِمْ بِالْمُشَفَّعْ

يا رَبِّ صَـلِّ عَـلَيْهِ وَسَلِّمْ

O Lord make our end be with the Intercessor
O Lord convey blessings and peace upon him

السَّلَامُ عَلَى رَسُولِ اللهِ ﷺ

Greetings upon the Prophet ﷺ

يَانَبِي سَلَامٌ عَلَيْكَ يَارَسُوْلُ سَلَامٌ عَلَيْكَ
يَاحَبِيْبُ سَلَامٌ عَلَيْكَ صَلَوَاتُ اللّٰه عَلَيْكَ

O Prophet, peace be upon you, O Messenger, peace be upon you
O Beloved, peace be upon you, may the blessings of Allah be upon you

اَشْرَقَ الْبَدْرُ عَلَيْنَا فَاخْتَفَتْ مِنْهُ الْبُدُوْرُ
مِثْلَ حُسْنِكْ مَارَاَيْنَا قَطُّ يَاوَجْهَ السُّرُوْرِ

The full moon has risen over us, by which the others have been eclipsed
Your beauty's like we have never seen, at all, O felicitous of face

اَنْتَ شَمْسٌ اَنْتَ بَدْرٌ اَنْتَ نُوْرٌ فَوْقَ نُوْرٍ
اَنْتَ اِكْسِيْرٌ وَّغَالِي اَنْتَ مِصْبَاحُ الصُّدُوْرِ

You are the sun and you are the moon, you are a light which is beyond light
You are the elixir but more precious, you are the lantern of breasts

يَاحَبِيْبِيْ يَا مُحَمَّدَ يَاعَرُوْسَ الْخَافِقَيْنِ

يَامُؤَيَّدْ يَامُمَجَّدْ يَاإِمَامَ الْقِبْلَتَيْنِ

O my beloved O Muhammad, the adoration of the East and West
O Support O Majestic, O Imam of the two qiblas

مَنْ رَّاٰى وَجْهَكَ يَسْعَدُ يَاكَرِيْمَ الْوَالِدَيْنِ

حَوْضُكَ الصَّافِي الْمُبَرَّدْ وِرْدُنَا يَوْمَ النُّشُوْرِ

The one who sees your face is joyous, O the one of noble parents
Your Hawd is pure and cool, our drink on the Day of Resurrection

مَارَاَيْنَا الْعِيْسَ حَنَّتْ بِالسُّرٰى اِلَّا اِلَيْكَ

وَالْغَمَامَةُ قَدْ اَظَلَّتْ وَالْمَلَا صَلُّوْا عَلَيْكَ

I have not seen the yearning of the camel, to travel by night except for you
And so the shading clouds have gathered over head, and the Highest Assembly sends blessings upon you

وَاَتَاكَ الْعُوْدُ يَبْكِيْ وَتَذَلَّلْ بَيْنَ يَدَيْكَ

وَاسْتَجَارَتْ يَاحَبِيْبِيْ عِنْدَكَ الظَّبْيُ النُّفُوْرُ

The withered trunk came to you crying, in submission before you
And she took refuge in you; my beloved, a shy and fearful gazelle

عِنْـدَمَاشَدُّ واالمَـحَامِلَ   وَتَـــنَادَوْ الِلرَّحِــيلِ

جِئْـتُهُمْ وَالدَّمْعُ سَــائِلَ   لِيْ يَادَلِيْــلِ قُلْتُ قِفْ

And when the caravan is ready, and they have called for the departure
I came to them my tears streaming, and said, ‘Wait for me!’ O guide

وَتَحَـمَّلْ لِّيْ رَسَــآئِلْ   اَيُّهَا الشَّــوْقُ الْجَزِيْلُ

نَحْـوَهَاتِـيكَ الْمَــنَازِلِ   فِي الْعَــشِيّ وَالْبُـكُورِ

Carry these letters on my behalf, O how much is the force of yearning
Take them towards those residences, in every eve and every morning

هَامُوْا الْكَوْنِ فِي مَنْ كُلُّ   فِــيكَ يَابَاهِيْ الْجَبِيْنِ

وَلَـهُمْ فِـيكَ غَــرَامٌ   وَاشْـتِيَاقٌ وَّحَــنِيْنُ

Everyone in the creation are in rapture, over you; O dazzling of face
And they are in love with you, restless and yearning

فِيْ مَعَانِــــيكَ الاَ نَامُ   قَدْ تَبَدَّتْ حَــائِرِيْنَ

اَنْتَ لِلرُّسُـلِ خِــتَامٌ   اَنْتَ لِلْمَــوْلٰى شَــكُوْرُ

Over your wonders are mankind in perplexion
You are the seal to all messengers, and to your Lord, you are grateful

عَبْدُكَ الْمِسْكِينُ يَرْجُو   فَضْلَكَ الْجَمَّ الْغَفِيرَ

فِيكَ قَدْ اَحْسَنْتُ ظَنِّي   يَابَشِيرُ يَانَذِيرُ

Your needy slave is in hope, for your effulgent and copious bounty
Regarding you, I have made my opinion beautiful,
O Bringer of gladness, O Warner

فَاَغِثْنِي وَاَجِرْنِي   يَامُجِيرُ مِنَ السَّعِيرِ

يَاغِيَاثِي يَامَلَاذِي   فِي مُهِمَّاتِ الْاُمُورِ

So help me and save me, O refuge from wretchedness
O Aid and sanctuary, in every time of concern

سَعِدَ عَبْدٌ قَدْ تَمَلَّى   وَانْجَلٰى عَنْهُ الْحَزِيْنُ

فِيكَ يَابَدْرُ تَجَلَّى   الْحَسِيْنُ فَلَكَ الْوَصْفُ

It is now that the slave is in joy, for sadness has been removed
And within you the moon is manifest, for you have the most beautiful description

لَيْسَ اَزْكٰى مِنْكَ اَصْلًا   قَطُّ يَاجَدَّ الْحُسَيْنِ

فَعَلَيْكَ اللّٰهُ صَلَّ   دَآئِمًا طُولَ الدُّهُورِ

There is no one more pure than you in origin, At all, O Grandfather of Hussayn,
For Allah sends blessings upon you, in all eternity and throughout time

يَـاوَلِيَّ الْحَـــسَنَاتِ   يَارَفِـيْعَ الدَّرَجَـاتِ

كَفِّرْ عَـنِّى الذُّنُـوْبَ   وَاغْـفِرْ عَنِّى السَّيِّـئَاتِ

O Awarder of good, O Elevator of rank
Expiate from me my sins, and forgive my wrongs

اَنْتَ غَـفَّارُ الْخَـطَايَا   وَالذُّنُـوْبِ الْمُـوْبِقَاتِ

اَنْتَ سَـتَّارُ الْمَسَاوِيْ   وَمُقِـيْلُ الْعَـــثَرَاتِ

For You are the Forgiver of mistakes, and of ruinous sins
You are the Veiler of wrongs and the Warner of pitfalls

عَالِـمُ السِّـرِّ وَاَخْـفٰى   مُسْتَجِـيْبُ الدَّعَوَاتِ

رَبِّ فَارْحَـمْنَا جَـمِيْعًا   وَامْـحُ عَنَّاالسَّـيِّئَاتِ

The Knower of the Secret and further hidden, the Answerer of supplications
Lord, have mercy upon us all, and cleanse wrong from us

رَبِّ فَارْحَـمْنَا جَـمِيْعًا   بِجَــمِيْعِ الصَّالِحَـاتِ

Lord have mercy upon us all, for the sake of the righteous

يا حبيب الله

يا رسول الله

(اَللّٰهُمَّ) اجْعَلْنَا لِآلَائِكَ ذَاكِرِينَ ، وَلِنَعْمَائِكَ شَاكِرِينَ ، وَلِيَوْمِ لِقَائِكَ مِنَ الذَّاكِرِينَ ، وَ أَحْيِنَا بِطَاعَتِكَ مَشْغُولِينَ ، وَإِذَا تَوَفَّيْتَنَا فَتَوَفَّنَا غَيْرَ مَفْتُونِينَ ، وَلَا مَخْذُولِينَ ، وَاخْتِمْ لَنَا مِنْكَ بِخَيْرٍ أَجْمَعِينَ ، (اَللّٰهُمَّ) اكْفِنَا شَرَّ الظَّالِمِينَ وَ اجْعَلْنَا مِنْ فِتْنَةِ هَذِهِ الدُّنْيَا سَالِمِينَ ، (اَللّٰهُمَّ) اجْعَلْ هَذَا الرَّسُولَ الْكَرِيمَ لَنَا شَفِيعًا ، وَارْزُقْنَا يَوْمَ الْقِيَامَةِ مَقَامًا رَفِيعًا ، (اَللّٰهُمَّ) اسْقِنَا مِنْ حَوْضِ نَبِيِّكَ مُحَمَّدٍ صَلَّى اللهُ عَلَيْهِ وَسَلَّمَ شَرْبَةً هَنِيئَةً لَا نَظْمَأُ بَعْدَهَا أَبَدًا ، وَاحْشُرْنَا تَحْتَ لِوَائِهِ غَدًا ، (اَللّٰهُمَّ) اغْفِرْ لَنَا بِهِ ، وَلِآبَائِنَا وَلِأُمَّهَاتِنَا ، وَمَشَايِخِنَا وَلِمُعَلِّمِينَا ، وَذَوِي الْحُقُوقِ عَلَيْنَا ، وَلِمَنْ أَجْرَى هَذِهِ الْخَيْرَ فِي هَذِهِ السَّاعَةِ ، وَلِجَمِيعِ الْمُؤْمِنِينَ وَالْمُؤْمِنَاتِ ، وَالْمُسْلِمِينَ وَالْمُسْلِمَاتِ ، اَلْأَحْيَاءِ مِنْهُمْ وَ الْأَمْوَاتِ ، إِنَّكَ مُجِيبُ الدَّعَوَاتِ وَقَاضِي الْحَاجَاتِ ، وَغَافِرُ الذُّنُوبِ وَالْخَطِيئَاتِ ، يَا أَرْحَمَ الرَّاحِمِينَ ، وَصَلَّى اللهُ عَلَى سَيِّدِنَا مُحَمَّدٍ وَعَلَى آلِهِ وَصَحْبِهِ وَسَلَّمَ وَالْحَمْدُ لِلّٰهِ رَبِّ الْعَالَمِينَ ، سُبْحَانَ رَبِّكَ رَبِّ الْعِزَّةِ عَمَّا يَصِفُونَ وَ سَلَامٌ عَلَى الْمُرْسَلِينَ وَالْحَمْدُ لِلّٰهِ رَبِّ الْعَالَمِينَ ۝

بسم الله الرحمن الرحيم

اَلْحَمْدُ لِلّٰهِ رَبِّ الْعَالَمِيْنَ (اَللّٰهُمَّ) صَلِّ وَسَلِّمْ عَلٰى سَيِّدِنَا مُحَمَّدٍ وَعَلٰى آلِهِ وَ صَحْبِهِ أَجْمَعِيْنَ ، جَعَلَنِى اللهُ وَ إِيَّاكُمْ مِمَّنْ يَسْتَوْجِبُ شَفَاعَتَهُ وَ يَرْجُوْ بِذٰلِكَ رَحْمَتَهُ وَ رَأْفَتَهُ ، (اَللّٰهُمَّ) بِحُرْمَةِ هٰذَا النَّبِيِّ الْكَرِيْمِ ، وَ آلِهِ الطَّاهِرِيْنَ ، وَ أَصْحَابِهِ السَّالِكِيْنَ ، عَلٰى نَهْجِهِ الْقَوِيْمِ ، اِجْعَلْنَا مِنْ خِيَارِ أُمَّتِهِ ، وَاسْتُرْنَا بِذَيْلِ حُرْمَتِهِ ، وَ احْشُرْنَا غَدًا فِي زُمْرَتِهِ ، وَاسْتَعْمِلْ أَلْسِنَتَنَا فِي مَدْحِهِ وَنُصْرَتِهِ ، وَأَحْيِنَا مُتَمَسِّكِيْنَ بِسُنَّتِهِ وَطَاعَتِهِ ، وَأَمِتْنَا عَلٰى حُبِّهِ وَ جَمَاعَتِهِ ، (اَللّٰهُمَّ) أَدْخِلْنَا مَعَهُ الْجَنَّةَ فَإِنَّهُ أَوَّلُ مَنْ يَدْخُلُهَا ، وَأَنْزِلْنَا مَعَهُ فِي قُصُوْرِهَا فَإِنَّهُ أَوَّلُ مَنْ يَنْزِلُهَا ، وَارْحَمْنَا يَوْمَ يَشْفَعُ لِلْخَلَائِقِ فَتَرْحَمُهَا ، (اَللّٰهُمَّ) ارْزُقْنَا زِيَارَتَهُ فِي كُلِّ حِيْنٍ ، وَلَا تَجْعَلْنَا مِنَ الْغَافِلِيْنَ عَنْكَ وَلَا عَنْهُ قَدْرَسِنه ، (اَللّٰهُمَّ) لَا تَجْعَلْ فِي مَجْلِسِنَا هٰذَا اَحَدًا إِلَّا غَسَلْتَ بِمَاءِ التَّوْبَةِ ذُنُوْبَه ، وَسَتَرْتَ بِرِدَاءِ الْمَغْفِرَةِ عُيُوبَه ، (اَللّٰهُمَّ) إِنَّهُ كَانَ مَعَنَا فِي السَّنَةِ الْمَاضِيَةِ إِخْوَانٌ مَنَعَهُمُ الْقَضَاءُ مِنَ الْوُصُوْلِ إِلَى مِثْلِهَا ، فَلَا تَحْرِمْهُمْ ثَوَابَ هٰذِهِ اللَّيْلَةِ وَ فَضْلِهَا ، (اَللّٰهُمَّ) ارْحَمْنَا إِذَا صِرْنَا مِنْ أَصْحَابِ الْقُبُوْرِ ، وَوَفِّقْنَا لِعَمَلٍ صَالِحٍ يَبْقٰى سَنَاهُ عَلٰى مَرِّ الدُّهُوْرِ

وَبِكَ اسْتَنَارَ الْكَوْنُ يَا عَلَمَ الْهُدَى

بِالنُّورِ وَالْإِنْعَامِ وَالْإِفْضَالِ

صَلَّى عَلَيْكَ اللهُ رَبِّي دَائِماً

أَبَداً مَعَ الْإِبْكَارِ وَالْآصَالِ

وَعَلَى جَمِيعِ الْآلِ وَالْأَصْحَابِ مَنْ

قَدْ خَصَّهُمْ رَبُّ الْعُلَى بِكَمَالِ

اللَّهُمَّ صَلِّ وَسَلِّمْ وَبَارِكْ عَلَيْهِ

وَمَا عَسَى أَنْ يُقَالَ فِيمَنْ وَصَفَهُ الْقُرْآنُ ۝ وَأَعْرَبَ عَنْ فَضَائِلِهِ التَّوْرَاةُ وَالْإِنْجِيلُ وَالزَّبُورُ وَالْفُرْقَانُ ۝ وَجَمَعَ اللهُ لَهُ بَيْنَ رُؤْيَتِهِ وَكَلَامِهِ ۝ وَقَرَنَ اسْمَهُ مَعَ اسْمِهِ تَنْبِيهاً عَلَى عُلُوِّ مَقَامِهِ ۝ وَجَعَلَهُ رَحْمَةً لِلْعَالَمِينَ وَنُوراً ۝ وَمَلَأَ بِمَوْلِدِهِ الْقُلُوبَ سُرُوراً ۝

اللَّهُمَّ صَلِّ وَسَلِّمْ وَبَارِكْ عَلَيْهِ

يَا بَدْرَ تِمٍّ حَازَ كُلَّ كَمَالِ

مَاذَا يُعَبِّرُ عَنْ عُلَاكَ مَقَالِي

أَنْتَ الَّذِي أَشْرَقْتَ فِي أُفُقِ الْعُلَى

فَمَحَوْتَ بِالْأَنْوَارِ كُلَّ ضَلَالِ

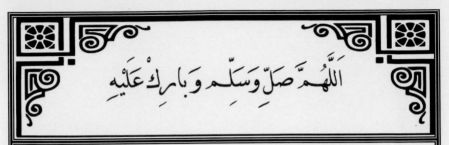

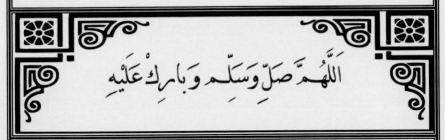

اللَّهُمَّ صَلِّ وَسَلِّمْ وَبَارِكْ عَلَيْهِ

وَقِيلَ لِبَعْضِهِمْ: كَأَنَّ وَجْهَهُ الْقَمَرُ، فَقَالَ: بَلْ أَضْوأُ مِنَ الْقَمَرِ إِذَا لَمْ يَحُلْ دُونَهُ الْغَمَامُ قَدْ غَشِيَهُ الْجَلَالُ ۞ وَانْتَهَى إِلَيْهِ الْكَمَالُ ۞ قَالَ بَعْضُ وَاصِفِيهِ: مَا رَأَيْتُ قَبْلَهُ وَلَا بَعْدَهُ مِثْلَهُ ۞ فَيَعْجِزُ لِسَانُ الْبَلِيغِ إِذَا أَرَادَ أَنْ يُحْصِيَ فَضْلَهُ ۞ فَسُبْحَانَ مَنْ خَصَّهُ صَلَّى اللهُ عَلَيْهِ وَسَلَّمَ بِالْمَحَلِّ الْأَسْنَى ۞ وَأَسْرَى بِهِ إِلَى قَابَ قَوْسَيْنِ أَوْ أَدْنَى ۞ وَأَيَّدَهُ بِالْمُعْجِزَاتِ الَّتِي لَا تُحْصَى ۞ وَوَافَاهُ مِنْ خِصَالِ الْكَمَالِ بِمَا يَجِلُّ أَنْ يُسْتَقْصَى ۞ وَأَعْطَاهُ خَمْساً لَمْ يُعْطِهِنَّ أَحَداً قَبْلَهُ ۞ وَآتَاهُ جَوَامِعَ الْكَلِمِ فَلَمْ يُدْرِكْ أَحَدٌ فَضْلَهُ ۞ وَكَانَ لَهُ صَلَّى اللهُ عَلَيْهِ وَسَلَّمَ فِي كُلِّ مَقَامٍ مَقَالٌ ۞ وَلِكُلِّ كَمَالٍ مِنْهُ كَمَالٌ ۞ لَا يَحُولُ فِي سُؤَالٍ وَلَا جَوَابٍ ۞ وَلَا يَجُولُ لِسَانُهُ إِلَّا فِي صَوَابٍ ۞

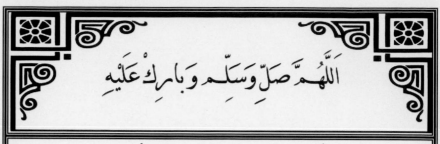

وَيُوجَدُ مِنهُ أَحسَنُ طِيبٍ وَأَن لَمْ يَكُن قَد تَطَيَّبَ ○ وَإِذَا مَشَى بَيْنَ أَصحَابِهِ فَكَأَنَّهُ القَمَرُ بَيْنَ النُّجُومِ الزُّهرِ ○ وَإِذَا أَقبَلَ لَيلاً فَكَأَنَّ النَّاسَ مِن نُورِهِ فِي أَوَانِ الظُّهرِ ○ وَكَانَ صَلَّى اللهُ عَلَيهِ وَسَلَّمَ أَجوَدَ بِالخَيرِ مِنَ الرِّيحِ المُرسَلَه ○ وَكَانَ يَرفُقُ بِاليَتِيمِ وَالأَرمَلَه ○ يَقُولُ بَعضُ وَاصِفِيهِ: مَا رَأَيتُ مِن ذِي لِمَّةٍ سَودَاءَ فِي حُلَّةٍ حَمرَاءَ ○ أَحسَنَ مِن رَسُولِ اللهِ صَلَّى اللهُ عَلَيهِ وَسَلَّمَ ○

اللَّهُمَّ صَلِّ وَسَلِّمْ وَبَارِكْ عَلَيْهِ

وَكَانَ صَلَّى اللهُ عَلَيْهِ وَسَلَّمَ أَحْسَنَ النَّاسِ خَلْقاً وَخُلُقاً ۞ وَأَهْدَاهُمْ إِلَى الْحَقِّ طُرُقًا وَكَانَ خُلُقُهُ الْقُرْآن ۞ وَشِيمَتُهُ الْغُفْرَان ۞ يَنْصَحُ لِلإِنْسَان ۞ وَيَفْسَحُ فِي الإِحْسَان وَيَعْفُو عَنِ الذَّنْبِ إِذَا كَانَ فِي حَقِّهِ وَسَبَبِه ۞ وَإِذَا أُضِيعَ حَقُّ اللهِ لَمْ يَقُمْ أَحَدٌ لِغَضَبِه ۞ مَنْ رَآهُ بَدِيهَةً هَابَه ۞ وَإِذَا دَعَاهُ الْمِسْكِينُ أَجَابَه ۞ يَقُولُ الْحَقَّ وَلَوْ كَانَ مُرًّا ۞ وَلَا يُضْمِرُ مُسْلِمٍ غِشًّا وَلَا ضُرًّا ۞ مَنْ نَظَرَ فِي وَجْهِهِ عَلِمَ أَنَّهُ لَيْسَ بِوَجْهِ كَذَّاب ۞ وَكَانَ صَلَّى اللهُ عَلَيْهِ وَسَلَّمَ لَيْسَ بِغَمَّازٍ وَلَا عَيَّاب ۞ إِذَا سُرَّ فَكَأَنَّ وَجْهَهُ قِطْعَةُ قَمَر ۞ وَإِذَا كَلَّمَ النَّاسَ فَكَأَنَّمَا يَجْنُونَ مِنْ كَلَامِهِ أَحْلَى ثَمَر وَإِذَا تَبَسَّمَ تَبَسَّمَ عَنْ مِثْلِ حَبِّ الْغَمَام ۞ وَإِذَا تَكَلَّمَ فَكَأَنَّمَا الدُّرَرُ يَسْقُطُ مِنْ ذَلِكَ الْكَلَام ۞ وَإِذَا تَحَدَّثَ فَكَأَنَّ الْمِسْكَ يَخْرُجُ مِنْ فِيهِ ۞ وَإِذَا مَرَّ بِطَرِيقٍ عُرِفَ مِنْ طِيبِهِ أَنَّهُ قَدْ مَرَّ فِيهِ ۞ وَإِذَا جَلَسَ فِي مَجْلِسٍ بَقِيَ طِيبُه فِيهِ أَيَّاماً وَإِنْ تَغَيَّب ۞

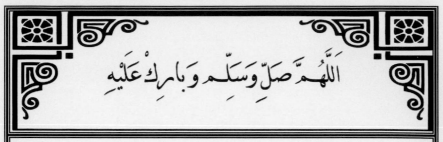

اَللّٰهُمَّ صَلِّ وَسَلِّمْ وَبَارِكْ عَلَيْهِ

فَبَيْنَمَا هُوَ ذَاتَ يَوْمٍ نَاءٍ عَنِ الأَوْطَان ۝ إِذْ أَقْبَلَ عَلَيْهِ ثَلاَثَةُ نَفَرٍ كَأَنَّ وُجُوهَهُمُ الشَّمْسُ وَالقَمَر ۝ فَانْطَلَقَ الصِّبْيَانُ هَرَبًا ۝ وَوَقَفَ النَّبِيُّ صَلَّى اللهُ عَلَيْهِ وَسَلَّمَ مُتَعَجِّباً ۝ فَأَضْجَعُوهُ عَلَى الأَرْضِ إِضْجَاعاً خَفِيفاً ۝ وَشَقُّوا بَطْنَهُ شَقًّا لَطِيفاً ۝ ثُمَّ أَخْرَجُوا قَلْبَ سَيِّدِ وَلَدِ عَدْنَان ۝ وَشَرَحُوهُ بِسِكِّينِ الإِحْسَانِ ۝ وَنَزَعُوا مِنْهُ حَظَّ الشَّيْطَان ۝ وَمَلَؤُوهُ بِالْحِلْمِ وَالْعِلْمِ وَالْيَقِينِ وَالرِّضْوَانِ ۝ وَأَعَادُوهُ إِلَى مَكَانِهِ ۝ فَقَامَ الحَبِيبُ صَلَّى اللهُ عَلَيْهِ وَسَلَّمَ سَوِيًّا كَمَا كَانَ ۝

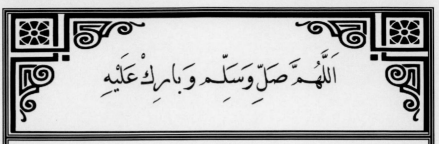

اللَّهُمَّ صَلِّ وَسَلِّمْ وَبَارِكْ عَلَيْهِ

فَلَمَّا أَعْرَضَ عَنْهُ مَرَاضِعُ الإِنْسِ ۝ لِمَا سَبَقَ فِي طَيِّ الغَيْبِ مِنَ السَّعَادَةِ

لِحَلِيمَةَ بِنْتِ أَبِي ذُؤَيْب ۝ فَلَمَّا وَقَعَ نَظَرُهَا عَلَيْهِ ۝ بَادَرَتْ مُسْرِعَةً إِلَيْه ۝

وَوَضَعَتْهُ فِي حِجْرِهَا وَضَمَّتْهُ إِلَى صَدْرِهَا ۝ فَهَشَّ لَهَا مُتَبَسِّمَا ۝

فَخَرَجَ مِنْ ثَغْرِهِ نُورٌ لَحِقَ بِالسَّمَا ۝ فَحَمَلَتْهُ إِلَى رَحْلِهَا ۝ وَارْتَحَلَتْ بِهِ إِلَى

أَهْلِهَا ۝ فَلَمَّا وَصَلَتْ بِهِ إِلَى مُقَامِهَا ۝ عَايَنَتْ بَرَكَتَهُ عَلَى أَغْنَامِهَا ۝

وَكَانَتْ كُلَّ يَوْمٍ تَرَى مِنْهُ بُرْهَانَا ۝ وَتَرْفَعُ لَهُ قَدْرًا وَشَانَا حَتَّى انْدَرَجَ فِي

حُلَّةِ اللُّطْفِ وَالأَمَان ۝ وَدَخَلَ بَيْنَ إِخْوَتِهِ مَعَ الصِّبْيَان ۝

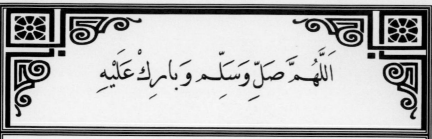

اَللَّهُمَّ صَلِّ وَسَلِّمْ وَبَارِكْ عَلَيْهِ

قِيلَ: مَنْ يَّكْفُلُ هَذِهِ الدُّرَّةَ اليَتِيمَهْ ۝ الَّتِي لَا تُوجَدُ لَهَا القِيمَهْ؟ قَالَتِ الطُّيُورُ: نَحْنُ نَكْفُلُهُ وَنَغْتَنِمُ هِمَّتَهُ العَظِيمَةْ ۝ قَالَتِ الوُحُوشُ: نَحْنُ أَوْلَى بِذَلِكَ لِكَيْ نَنَالَ شَرَفَهُ وَتَعْظِيمَهْ ۝ قِيلَ: يَا مَعْشَرَ الأُمَمِ أُسْكُتُوا، فَإِنَّ اللهَ قَدْ حَكَمَ فِي سَابِقِ حِكْمَتِهِ القَدِيمَةْ ۝ بِأَنَّ نَبِيَّهُ مُحَمَّدًا صَلَّى اللهُ عَلَيْهِ وَسَلَّمَ يَكُونُ رَضِيعاً لِحَلِيمَةَ الحَلِيمَةْ ۝

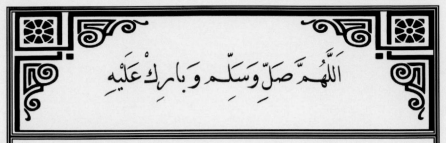

وَوُلِدَ صَلَّى اللهُ عَلَيْهِ وَسَلَّمَ مَخْتُوناً بِيَدِ الْعِنَايَه ۝ مَكْحُولاً بِكُحْلِ الْهِدَايَه ۝ فَأَشْرَقَ بِبَهَائِهِ الْفَضَا ۝ وَتَلأْلأَ الْكَوْنُ مِنْ نُورِهِ وَأَضَا ۝ وَدَخَلَ فِي عَقْدِ بَيْعَتِهِ مَنْ بَقِيَ مِنَ الْخَلَائِقِ كَمَا دَخَلَ فِيهَا مَنْ مَضَى ۝ أَوَّلُ فَضِيلَةِ الْمُعْجِزَاتُ بِخُمُودِ نَارِ فَارِس وَسُقُوطِ الشُّرُفَات ۝ وَرُمِيَتِ الشَّيَاطِينُ مِنَ السَّمَاءِ بِالشُّهُبِ الْمُحْرِقَات ۝ وَرَجَعَ كُلُّ جَبَّارٍ مِنَ الْجِنِّ وَهُوَ بِصَوْلَةِ سَلْطَنَتِهِ ذَلِيلٌ خَاضِع ۝ لَمَّا تَأَلَّقَ مِنْ سَنَاهُ النُّورُ السَّاطِع ۝ وَأَشْرَقَ مِنْ بَهَائِهِ الضِّيَاءُ اللَّامِع ۝ حَتَّى عُرِضَ عَلَى الْمَرَاضِع ۝

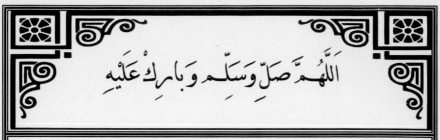

اللَّهُمَّ صَلِّ وَسَلِّمْ وَبَارِكْ عَلَيْهِ

فَاهْتَزَّ الْعَرْشُ طَرَباً وَاسْتِبْشَارًا ۝ وَازْدَادَ الْكُرْسِيُّ هَيْبَةً وَ وَقَارًا ۝

وَامْتَلأَتِ السَّمَاوَاتُ أَنْوَارًا ۝ وَضَجَّتِ الْمَلائِكَةُ تَهْلِيلاً وَ تَمْجِيدًا

وَاسْتِغْفَارًا ۝ وَلَمْ تَزَلْ أُمُّهُ تَرَى أَنْوَاعاً مِنْ فَخْرِهِ وَفَضْلِه ۝ إِلَى نِهَايَةِ

تَمَامِ حَمْلِه ۝ فَلَمَّا اشْتَدَّ بِهَا الطَّلْقُ بِإِذْنِ رَبِّ الْخَلْقِ وَضَعَتِ الْحَبِيبَ صَلَّى

اللهُ عَلَيْهِ وَسَلَّمَ ، سَاجِدًا شَاكِرًا حَامِدًا كَأَنَّهُ الْبَدْرُ فِي تَمَامِهِ ۝

(هنا محل القيام)

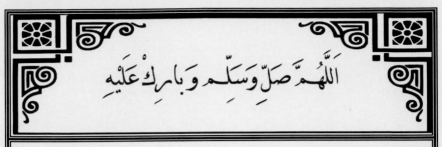

اَللَّهُمَّ صَلِّ وَسَلِّمْ وَبَارِكْ عَلَيْهِ

أَحْضِرُوا قُلُوبَكُمْ يَا مَعْشَرَ ذَوِى الْأَلْبَابِ حَتَّى أَجْلُوَلَكُمْ عَرَائِسَ مَعَانِي

أَجَلِّ الْأَحْبَابِ ۞ الْمَخْصُوصِ بِأَشْرَفِ الْأَلْقَابِ ۞ الرَّاقِي إِلَى حَضْرَةِ

الْمَلِكِ الْوَهَّابِ ۞ حَتَّى نَظَرَ إِلَى جَمَالِهِ بِلَا سِتْرٍ وَلَا حِجَابٍ ۞ فَلَمَّا آنَ أَوَانُ

ظُهُورِ شَمْسِ الرِّسَالَةِ فِي سَمَاءِ الْجَلَالَةِ خَرَجَ بِهِ مَرْسُومُ الْجَلِيلِ ۞ لِنَقِيبِ

الْمَمْلَكَةِ جِبْرِيلَ ۞ يَا جِبْرِيلُ نَادِ فِي سَائِرِ الْمَخْلُوقَاتِ ۞ مِنْ أَهْلِ

الْأَرْضِ وَالسَّمَاوَاتِ ۞ بِالتَّهَانِي وَالْبِشَارَاتِ ۞ فَإِنَّ النُّورَ الْمَصُونَ ۞

وَالسِّرَّ الْمَكْنُونَ ۞ الَّذِي أَوْجَدْتُهُ قَبْلَ وُجُودِ الْأَشْيَاءِ ۞ وَإِبْدَاعِ الْأَرْضِ

وَالسَّمَاءِ ۞ أَنْقُلُهُ فِي هَذِهِ اللَّيْلَةِ إِلَى بَطْنِ أُمِّهِ مَسْرُورًا ۞ أَمْلَأُ بِهِ

الْكَوْنَ نُورًا ۞ أَكْفُلُهُ يَتِيمًا ۞ وَأُطَهِّرُهُ وَأَهْلَ بَيْتِهِ تَطْهِيرًا ۞

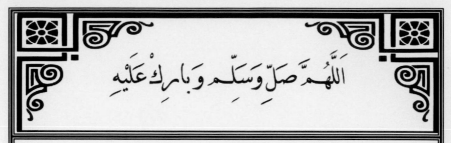

◯ فَيَقُولُ الْحَقُّ: وَعِزَّتِي وَجَلَالِي لَا جَعَلْتُ مَنْ أَخْلَصَ لِي بِالشَّهَادَةِ كَمَنْ

كَذَّبَ بِي، أَدْخِلُوهُمُ الْجَنَّةَ بِرَحْمَتِي ◯

اللَّهُمَّ صَلِّ وَسَلِّمْ وَبَارِكْ عَلَيْهِ

يَا أَعَزَّ جَوَاهِرِ الْعُقُودِ، وَخُلَاصَةَ إِكْسِيرِ سِرِّ الْوُجُودِ، مَادِحُكَ قَاصِرٌ وَلَوْ

جَاءَ بِبَذْلِ الْمَجْهُودِ، وَوَاصِفُكَ عَاجِزٌ عَنْ حَصْرِ مَا حَوَيْتَ مِنْ خِصَالِ

الْكَرَمِ وَالْجُودِ، الْكَوْنُ، إِشَارَةٌ وَأَنْتَ الْمَقْصُودُ ◯ يَا أَشْرَفَ مَنْ نَالَ الْمَقَامَ

الْمَحْمُودَ، وَجَاءَتْ رُسُلٌ مِنْ قَبْلِكَ لِكِنَّهُمْ بِالرِّفْعَةِ وَالْعُلَى لَكَ شُهُودٌ ◯

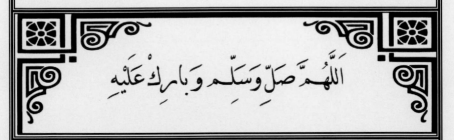

(الْحَدِيثُ الثَّانِي) عَنْ عَطَاءِ بْنِ يَسَارٍ عَنْ كَعْبِ الْأَحْبَارِ قَالَ: عَلَّمَنِي أَبِي التَّوْرَاةَ إِلَّا الْأَسْفَارَ وَاحِدًا كَانَ يَخْتِمُهُ وَيُدْخِلُهُ الصُّنْدُوقَ فَلَمَّا مَاتَ أَبِي فَتَحْتُهُ فَإِذَا فِيهِ: نَبِيٌّ يَخْرُجُ آخِرَ الزَّمَانِ ۞ مَوْلِدُهُ بِمَكَّةَ، وَهِجْرَتُهُ بِالْمَدِينَةِ، وَ سُلْطَانُهُ بِالشَّامِ يَقُصُّ شَعْرَهُ، وَيَتَّزِرُ عَلَى وَسَطِهِ ۞ يَكُونُ خَيْرَ الْأَنْبِيَاءِ، وَ أُمَّتُهُ خَيْرَ الْأُمَمِ ۞ يُكَبِّرُونَ اللهَ تَعَالَى عَلَى كُلِّ شَرَفٍ ۞ يَصُفُّونَ فِي الصَّلَاةِ كَصُفُوفِهِمْ فِي الْقِتَالِ ۞ قُلُوبُهُمْ مَصَاحِفُهُمْ يَحْمَدُونَ اللهَ تَعَالَى عَلَى كُلِّ شِدَّةٍ وَرَخَاءٍ ۞ ثُلُثٌ يَدْخُلُونَ الْجَنَّةَ بِغَيْرِ حِسَابٍ ۞ وَثُلُثٌ يَأْتُونَ بِذُنُوبِهِمْ وَخَطَايَاهُمْ فَيَغْفِرُ لَهُمْ ۞ وَثُلُثٌ يَأْتُونَ بِذُنُوبٍ وَخَطَايَا عِظَامٍ ۞ فَيَقُولُ اللهُ تَعَالَى لِلْمَلَائِكَةِ: اِذْهَبُوا فَزِنُوهُمْ، فَيَقُولُونَ: يَا رَبَّنَا وَجَدْنَاهُمْ أَسْرَفُوا عَلَى أَنْفُسِهِمْ، وَوَجَدْنَا أَعْمَالَهُمْ مِنَ الذُّنُوبِ كَأَمْثَالِ الْجِبَالِ، غَيْرَ أَنَّهُمْ يَشْهَدُونَ أَنْ لَا إِلٰهَ إِلَّا اللهُ وَأَنَّ مُحَمَّدًا رَسُولُ اللهِ صَلَّى اللهُ عَلَيْهِ وَسَلَّمَ

اللَّهُمَّ صَلِّ وَسَلِّمْ وَبَارِكْ عَلَيْهِ

(الحَدِيثُ الأوَّلُ): عَنْ بَحْرِ العِلْمِ الدَّافِقِ ۝ وَلِسَانِ القُرْآنِ النَّاطِقِ ۝ أَوْحَدِ عُلَمَاءِ النَّاسِ ۝ سَيِّدِنَا عَبْدَ اللهِ بْنِ سَيِّدِنَا العَبَّاسِ رَضِيَ اللهُ عَنْهُمَا عَنْ رَسُولِ اللهِ صَلَّى اللهُ عَلَيْهِ وَسَلَّمَ أَنَّهُ قَالَ: كُنْتُ نُوراً بَيْنَ يَدَيِ اللهِ عَزَّ وَجَلَّ قَبْلَ أَنْ يَخْلُقَ آدَمَ بِأَلْفَيْ عَامٍ يُسَبِّحُ اللهَ ذَلِكَ النُّورُ وَتُسَبِّحُ المَلَائِكَةُ بِتَسْبِيحِهِ ۝ فَلَمَّا خَلَقَ اللهُ آدَمَ أَلْقَى ذَلِكَ النُّورَ فِي طِينَتِهِ قَالَ صَلَّى اللهُ عَلَيْهِ وَسَلَّمَ: فَأَهْبَطَنِيَ اللهُ عَزَّ وَجَلَّ إِلَى الأَرْضِ فِي ظَهْرِ آدَمَ ۝ وَحَمَلَنِي فِي السَّفِينَةِ فِي صُلْبِ نُوحٍ ۝ وَجَعَلَنِي فِي صُلْبِ الخَلِيلِ إِبْرَاهِيمَ حِينَ قُذِفَ بِهِ فِي النَّارِ ۝ وَلَمْ يَزَلِ اللهُ عَزَّ وَجَلَّ يَنْقُلُنِي مِنَ الأَصْلَابِ الطَّاهِرَةِ إِلَى الأَرْحَامِ الزَّكِيَّةِ الفَاخِرَةِ ۝ حَتَّى أَخْرَجَنِيَ اللهُ مِنْ بَيْنِ أَبَوَيَّ وَهُمَا لَمْ يَلْتَقِيَا عَلَى سِفَاحٍ قَطُّ ۝

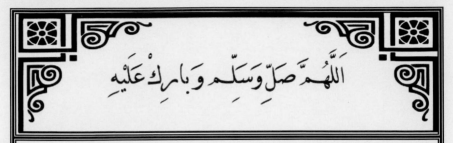

اللَّهُمَّ صَلِّ وَسَلِّمْ وَبَارِكْ عَلَيْهِ

أَوَّلُ مَا نَسْتَفْتِحُ بِإِيرَادِ حَدِيثَيْنِ وَرَدَا عَنْ نَبِيٍّ كَانَ قَدْرُهُ عَظِيمًا ○ وَنَسَبُهُ كَرِيمًا ○ وَصِرَاطُهُ مُسْتَقِيمًا ○ قَالَ فِي حَقِّهِ مَنْ لَمْ يَزَلْ سَمِيعًا عَلِيمًا:

﴿إِنَّ اللَّهَ وَمَلَائِكَتَهُ يُصَلُّونَ عَلَى النَّبِيِّ

يَا أَيُّهَا الَّذِينَ آمَنُوا صَلُّوا عَلَيْهِ وَسَلِّمُوا تَسْلِيمًا﴾

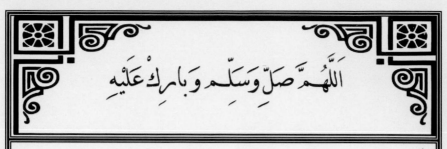

اللَّهُمَّ صَلِّ وَسَلِّمْ وَبَارِكْ عَلَيْهِ

فَسُبْحَانَ مَنْ خَصَّهُ صَلَّى اللهُ عَلَيْهِ وَسَلَّمَ بِأَشْرَافِ الْمَنَاصِبِ وَالْمَرَاتِبِ ۝ أَحْمَدُهُ عَلَى مَا مَنَحَ مِنَ الْمَوَاهِبِ ۝ وَأَشْهَدُ أَنْ لَّا إِلٰهَ إِلَّا اللهُ وَحْدَهُ لَا شَرِيكَ لَهُ رَبُّ الْمَشَارِقِ وَالْمَغَارِبِ ۝ وَأَشْهَدُ أَنَّ سَيِّدَنَا مُحَمَّدًا عَبْدُهُ وَرَسُولُهُ الْمَبْعُوثُ إِلَى سَائِرِ الْأَعَاجِمِ وَالْأَعَارِبِ ۝ صَلَّى اللهُ عَلَيْهِ وَعَلَى آلِهِ وَأَصْحَابِهِ أُولى الْمَآثِرِ وَالْمَنَاقِبِ ۝ صَلَاةً وَسَلَامًا دَائِمَيْنِ مُتَلَازِمَيْنِ يَأْتِي قَائِلُهُمَا يَوْمَ الْقِيَامَةِ غَيْرَ خَائِبِ ۝

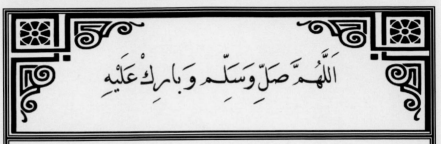

لَهُ الشَّـرَفُ المُؤَبَّدُ والمَـنَاقِبُ

فَلَوْ أَنَّا سَعَـيْنَا كُلَّ حِـيْنٍ

عَـلَى الأَحْـدَاقِ لاَ فَوْقَ النَّجَائِبُ

وَلَـوْ أَنَّا عَـمِلْنَا كُلَّ يَـوْمٍ

لأَحْـمَدَ مَـوْلِداً قَدْ كَانَ وَاجِـبُ

عَـلَيْهِ مِـنَ المُهَيْمِنِ كُلَّ وَقْتٍ

صَـلاَةٌ مَـا بَدَا نُورُ الكَوَاكِبُ

تَعُـمُّ الآلَ وَالأَصْـحَابَ طُـرًّا

جَمِـيْعَهُمُ وَعِـتْرَتَهُ الاَطَايِـبُ

قِبَابُ الحَيِّ لاَحَتْ وَالمَضَارِب

وَتِلْكَ القُبَّةُ الخَضْرَآءُ فِيهَا

نَبِيٌّ نُورُهُ يَجْلُو الغَيَاهِبْ

وَقَدْ صَحَّ الرِّضَا وَدَنَا التَّلاَقِي

وَقَدْ جَاءَ الهَنَا مِنْ كُلِّ جَانِبْ

فَقُلْ لِلنَّفْسِ دُونَكِ وَالتَّمَلِّي

فَمَا دُونَ الحَبِيبِ اليَومَ حَاجِبْ

تَمَلَّى بِالحَبِيبِ بِكُلِّ قَصْدٍ

فَقَدْ حَصَلَ الهَنَا وَالضِّدُّ غَائِبْ

نَبِيُّ اللهِ خَيْرُ الخَلْقِ جَمْعاً

لَهُ أَعْلَى المَنَاصِبِ وَالمَرَاتِبْ

لَـهُ الجَاهُ الرَّفِيعُ لَـهُ المَعَالِي

صَلَاةُ اللهِ مَا دَارَتْ كَوَاكِبْ

عَلَى اَحْمَدَ خَيْرِ مَنْ رَكِبَ النَّجَائِبْ

حَدَا حَادِى السُّرٰى بِاسْمِ الحَبَائِبْ

فَهَزَّ السُّكْرُ أَعْطَافَ الرَّكَائِبْ

أَلَمْ تَرَهَا وَقَدْ مَدَّتْ خُطَاهَا

وَسَالَتْ مِنْ مَدَامِعِهَا سَحَائِبْ

فَدَعْ جَذْبَ الزِّمَامِ وَلَا تَسُقْهَا

فَقَائِدُ شَوْقِهَا لِلْحَيِّ جَاذِبْ

فَهِمْ طَرَبًا كَمَا هَامَتْ وَإِلَّا

فَإِنَّكَ فِى طَرِيْقِ الْحُبِّ كَاذِبْ

أَمَا هٰذَا الْعَقِيْقُ بَدَا وَهٰذِى

الْعَالَمِينَ ۝ وَوَصَلَ إِلَى قَابَ قَوْسَيْنِ كُنْتُ لَهُ أَنَا النَّدِيمُ وَالْمُخَاطِبُ ۝

اللَّهُمَّ صَلِّ وَسَلِّمْ وَبَارِكْ عَلَيْهِ

ثُمَّ أَرُدُّهُ مِنَ الْعَرْشِ ۝ قَبْلَ أَنْ يَبْرُدَ الْفَرْشُ ۝ وَقَدْ نَالَ جَمِيعَ الْمَآرِبِ ۝ فَإِذَا شُرِّفَتْ تُرْبَةُ طَيْبَةَ مِنْهُ بِأَشْرَفِ قَالَبٍ ۝ سَعَتْ إِلَيْهِ أَرْوَاحُ الْمُحِبِّينَ عَلَى الْأَقْدَامِ وَالنَّجَائِبِ ۝

اللَّهُمَّ صَلِّ وَسَلِّمْ وَبَارِكْ عَلَيْهِ

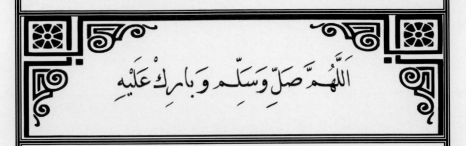

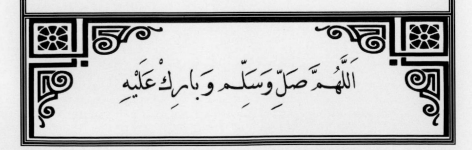

اللّٰهُمَّ صَلِّ وَسَلِّمْ وَبَارِكْ عَلَيْهِ

يُبْعَثُ مِنْ تِهَامَة ۞ بَيْنَ يَدَيِ الْقِيَامَة ۞ فِي ظَهْرِهِ عَلَامَة ۞
تُظِلُّهُ الغَمَامَه ۞ تُطِيعُهُ السَّحَائِب ۞ فَجْرِيُّ الجَبِينِ لَيْلِيُّ
الذَّوَائِب ۞ أَلِفِيُّ الأَنْفِ نُونِيُّ الحَاجِب ۞ سَمْعُهُ يَسْمَعُ صَرِيرَ
الْقَلَمِ بَصَرُهُ إِلَى السَّبْعِ الطِّبَاقِ ثَاقِب ۞ قَدَمَاهُ قَبَّلَهُمَا الْبَعِيرُ فَأَزَالَ مَا
اشْتَكَاهُ مِنَ الْمِحَنِ وَالنَّوَائِب ۞ آمَنَ بِهِ الضَّبُّ وَسَلَّمَتْ عَلَيْهِ
الأَشْجَارُ وَخَاطَبَتْهُ الأَحْجَارُ وَحَنَّ إِلَيْهِ الجِذْعُ حَنِينَ حَزِينٍ نَادِب ۞
يَدَاهُ تَظْهَرُ بَرَكَتُهُمَا فِي الْمَطَاعِمِ وَالْمَشَارِب ۞ قَلْبُهُ لَا يَغْفُلُ وَلَا
يَنَامُ وَلٰكِنْ لِلْخِدْمَةِ عَلَى الدَّوَامِ مُرَاقِب ۞ إِنْ أُوذِيَ يَعْفُ وَلَا يُعَاقِب ۞
وَإِنْ خُوصِمَ يَصْمُتُ وَلَا يُجَاوِب ۞ أَرْفَعُهُ إِلَى أَشْرَفِ الْمَرَاتِب ۞ فِي
رَكْبَةٍ لَا تَنْبَغِي قَبْلَهُ وَلَا بَعْدَهُ لِرَاكِب ۞ فِي مَوْكِبٍ مِنَ الْمَلَائِكَةِ
يَفُوقُ عَلَى سَائِرِ الْمَوَاكِب ۞ فَإِذَا ارْتَقَى عَلَى الْكَوْنَيْنِ وَانْفَصَلَ عَنِ

اَللّٰهُمَّ صَلِّ وَسَلِّمْ وَبَارِكْ عَلَيْهِ

قِيلَ: هُوَ آدَمُ ، قَالَ: آدَمُ بِهِ أُنِيلُهُ أَعْلَى الْمَرَاتِب ۝ قِيلَ: هُوَ نُوحٌ ، قَالَ: نُوحٌ بِهِ يَنْجُو مِنَ الْغَرَقِ وَ يَهْلِكُ مَنْ خَالَفَهُ مِنَ الأَهْلِ وَالأَقَارِب ۝ قِيلَ: هُوَ إِبْرَاهِيمُ ، قَالَ إِبْرَاهِيمُ: بِهِ تَقُومُ حُجَّتُهُ عَلَى عُبَّادِ الأَصْنَامِ وَالْكَوَاكِب ۝ قِيلَ: هُوَ مُوسَى ، قَالَ: مُوسَى أَخُوهُ وَلَكِنْ: هَذَا حَبِيبٌ وَمُوسَى كَلِيمٌ وَمُخَاطِب ۝ قِيلَ: هُوَ عِيسَى ، قَالَ: عِيسَى يُبَشِّرُ بِهِ وَهُوَ بَيْنَ يَدَيْ نُبُوَّتِهِ كَالْحَاجِب ۝

قِيلَ: فَمَنْ هَذَا الْحَبِيبُ الْكَرِيمُ الَّذِي أَلْبَسْتَهُ حُلَّةَ الْوَقَارِ ، وَتَوَّجْتَهُ بِتِيجَانِ الْمَهَابَةِ وَالإِفْتِخَار ۝ وَنَشَرْتَ عَلَى رَأْسِهِ الْعَصَائِب ۝ قَالَ: هُوَ نَبِيٌّ إِسْتَخَرْتُهُ مِنْ لُؤَيِّ بْنِ غَالِب ۝ يَمُوتُ أَبُوهُ وَأُمُّهُ وَ ثُمَّ مَّهُ الشَّقِيقُ أَبُو طَالِب ۝

فَلاَ يَزَالُونَ فِي الإِسْتِغْفَارِ حَتَّى يَكُفَّ كَفُّ النَّهَارِ ذُيُولَ
الغَيَاهِبِ ۝ فَيَعُودُونَ وَقَدْ فَازُوا بِالمَطْلُوبِ ۝ وَأَدْرَكُوا رِضَا
المَحْبُوبِ ۝ وَلَمْ يَعُدْ أَحَدٌ مِنَ القَوْمِ وَهُوَ خَائِبٌ ۝ (لا إله إلاّ الله)
فَسُبْحَانَهُ تَعَالَى مِنْ مَلِكٍ أَوْجَدَ نُورَ نَبِيِّهِ سَيِّدِنَا (مُحَمَّدٍ) صَلَّى اللهُ
عَلَيْهِ وَسَلَّمَ قَبْلَ أَنْ يَخْلُقَ آدَمَ مِنَ الطِّينِ اللاَّزِبِ ۝ وَعَرَضَ
فَخْرَهُ عَلَى الأَشْيَاءِ وَقَالَ: هَذَا سَيِّدُ الأَنْبِيَاءِ وَأَجَلُّ الأَصْفِيَاءِ وَأَكْرَمُ
الحَبَائِبِ ۝

بسم الله الرحمن الرحيم

اَلْحَمْدُ لِلّٰهِ الْقَوِيِّ الْغَالِبِ ۝ اَلْوَلِيِّ الطَّالِبِ ۝ اَلْبَاعِثِ الْمَانِحِ الْوَارِثِ السَّالِبِ ۝ عَالِمِ الْكَائِنِ وَالْبَائِنِ وَالزَّائِلِ وَالذَّاهِبِ ۝ يُسَبِّحُهُ الْآفِلُ وَالْمَائِلُ وَالطَّالِعُ وَالْغَارِبُ ۝ وَيُوَحِّدُهُ النَّاطِقُ وَالصَّامِتُ وَالْجَامِدُ وَالذَّآئِبُ ۝ يَضْرِبُ بِعَدْلِهِ السَّاكِنُ ۝ وَيَسْكُنُ بِفَضْلِهِ الضَّارِبُ ۝ (لا إله إلا الله) حَكِيمٌ أَظْهَرَ بَدِيعَ حِكَمِهِ وَالْعَجَائِبِ ۝ فِي تَرْتِيبِ تَرْكِيبِ هٰذِهِ الْقَوَالِبِ ۝ خَلَقَ مُخًّا وَّعَظْمًا وَّعَضَلًا وَّعُرُوقًا وَّلَحْمًا وَّجِلْدًا ۝ وَّشَعْرًا وَّدَمًا بِنَظْمٍ مُّؤْتَلِفٍ مُتَرَاكِبٍ ۝ مِنْ مَاءٍ دَافِقٍ يَّخْرُجُ مِنْ بَيْنِ الصُّلْبِ وَالتَّرَآئِبِ ۝ (لا إله إلا الله) كَرِيمٌ بَسَطَ لِخَلْقِهِ بِسَاطَ كَرَمِهِ وَالْمَوَاهِبِ ۝ يَنْزِلُ فِي كُلِّ لَيْلَةٍ إِلَى السَّمَاءِ الدُّنْيَا ۝ وَيُنَادِي: هَلْ مِنْ مُسْتَغْفِرٍ، هَلْ مِنْ تَائِبٍ ۝ هَلْ مِنْ طَالِبِ حَاجَةٍ فَأُنِيلَهُ الْمَطَالِبَ ۝ فَلَوْ رَأَيْتَ الْخُدَّامَ قِيَامًا عَلَى الْأَقْدَامِ وَقَدْ جَادُوا بِالدُّمُوعِ السَّوَاكِبِ ۝ وَالْقَوْمَ بَيْنَ نَادِمٍ وَتَائِبٍ ۝ وَخَائِفٍ لِنَفْسِهِ يُعَاتِبُ ۝ وَآبِقٍ مِنَ الذُّنُوبِ إِلَيْهِ هَارِبٍ ۝

Muḥammad Rasūlallāh

"Muhammad is the Messenger of Allah…"

[Quran, Al-Fatḥ:29]

[illegible]